WILLIAM FAULKNER

LIVES AND LEGACIES

Larzer Ziff
MARK TWAIN

David S. Reynolds
WALT WHITMAN

Edwin S. Gaustad
ROGER WILLIAMS
BENJAMIN FRANKLIN

Gale E. Christianson
ISAAC NEWTON

Paul Addison
WINSTON CHURCHILL

G. Edward White
OLIVER WENDELL HOLMES JR.

Craig Raine
T. S. ELIOT

Carolyn Porter
WILLIAM FAULKNER

WILLIAM FAULKNER

Carolyn Porter

OXFORD
UNIVERSITY PRESS

2007

OXFORD
UNIVERSITY PRESS

Oxford University Press, Inc., publishes works that further
Oxford University's objective of excellence
in research, scholarship, and education.

Oxford New York
Auckland Cape Town Dar es Salaam Hong Kong Karachi
Kuala Lumpur Madrid Melbourne Mexico City Nairobi
New Delhi Shanghai Taipei Toronto

With offices in
Argentina Austria Brazil Chile Czech Republic France Greece
Guatemala Hungary Italy Japan Poland Portugal Singapore
South Korea Switzerland Thailand Turkey Ukraine Vietnam

Copyright © 2007 by Carolyn Porter

Published by Oxford University Press, Inc.
198 Madison Avenue, New York, NY 10016
www.oup.com

Library of Congress Cataloging-in-Publication Data
Porter, Carolyn, 1946–
William Faulkner/Carolyn Porter.
p. cm.—(Lives and legacies)
Includes bibliographical references and index.
ISBN 978-0-19-531049-8
1. Faulkner, William, 1897–1962.
2. Novelists, American—20th century—Biography.
I. Title.
PS3511.A86Z946387 2007
813′.52—dc22
[B]
2006039181

1 3 5 7 9 8 6 4 2
Printed in the United States of America
on acid-free paper

To my guys, Charlie and George

CONTENTS

One

YOUTH AND APPRENTICESHIP:
THE SOUND AND THE FURY

The Long Beginning

FAULKNER'S LIFE WAS ALL ABOUT STORIES—MAKING THEM UP, making them over, even making them true. As a child in Oxford, Mississippi, he was a famous storyteller, often spinning tales with more verisimilitude than veracity. He was also an ardent listener, as he had learned to be from listening to family stories told by his grandfather, his aunts and uncles, his neighbors, stories that were themselves often more made-up than not. Meanwhile, people began to tell stories about Faulkner as well, especially as he grew up and became a writer. Once he acquired a reputation as a novelist, he came to enjoy provoking stories about himself and his past as well as telling them himself. Between the tales he told of himself and those told about him, his biographers have thus had rich treasures to draw upon in their effort to tell Faulkner's own story. Although they've done an admirable job of sorting truth from fiction, they have also

1

demonstrated that to understand Faulkner at all, one must take the stories at least as seriously as the so-called facts.

Consider for example the story Faulkner told when requested to provide an author's profile for *Forum*, which was to publish "A Rose for Emily," the first short story for which he was actually paid, in its April 1930 issue.

> Born male and single at early age in Mississippi. Quit school after five years in seventh grade. Got job in Grandfather's bank and learned medicinal value of his liquor. Grandfather thought janitor did it. Hard on janitor. War came. Liked British uniform. Got commission R.F.C. pilot. Crashed. Cost British gov't L2000. Was still pilot. Crashed. Cost British gov't L2000. Quit. Cost British gov't $83.40. King said, "Well done." Returned to Mississippi. Family got job: postmaster. Resigned by mutual agreement on part of two inspectors; accused of throwing all incoming mail into garbage can. How disposed of out-going mail never proved. Inspectors foiled. Had $700. Went to Europe. Met man named Sherwood Anderson. Said, "Why not write novels? Maybe won't have to work." Did. *Soldier's Pay*. Did. *Mosquitoes*. Did. *The Sound and the Fury*. Did *Sanctuary*, out next year. Now flying again. Age 32. Own and operate own typewriter.[1]

From the outset, it is clear that Faulkner is making fun of the implicit biographical form he has been asked to fill out. What follows is to be understood, therefore, as designed more to amuse than to inform. Faulkner was intensely devoted to his privacy and rarely provided straight answers to biographical questions. Instead, he took the opportunity to continue the fabrication of his life story, a creative project he had begun in earnest during his military stint. If we look at this mini-autobiography in the context of the knowable facts, we can readily identify some major omissions and distortions. For example, Faulkner quit school, finally, in the eleventh grade, as soon as football season ended, but he had been a star student in grammar school, skipping the second grade because of his obvious intelligence. His commission was in the Canadian Royal Air Force (CRAF), not the British Royal Flying Corps (BRFC), and the war ended before he completed training in Canada. His friend Phil Stone, not his family, actually secured the postmaster's job for him, although had he not been a Falkner (as the family name was spelled), he probably wouldn't have been able to get it. He did go to Europe, but before that he met Sherwood Anderson in New Orleans. Faulkner arrived there in January 1925 intending to go to Europe, but he found Anderson and the community of writers and artists associated with the literary journal, *The Double Dealer*, so engaging that he stayed on for six months, producing his first serious batch of prose and writing his first novel, *Soldier's Pay* (1926). Finally, he omits from his list of novels in print or in press *Sartoris*, a revision of his first Yoknapatawpha novel, published just the year before, in 1929.

Some of these facts matter more than others in our understanding of who Faulkner was, but to see how they matter, we need to approach the story Faulkner is telling here first as a story. That story is far more revealing than any corrected version of it could be.

Here is one way of reading this story. Faulkner portrays himself as failing at each task he assumes; he gets drunk rather than fulfill his duties in his grandfather's bank, he crashes an airplane twice, he can't deliver the mail properly. So, thanks to

Sherwood Anderson's model, and perhaps his advice, Faulkner takes up novel writing as an alternative to having "to work." This, he proudly announces, turns out to be something he can do. Look! He's done it again and again. He lists his works (getting in a plug for his novels), and adds that he is "flying again," signaling his recuperative powers, or perhaps his persistent foolhardiness. That he is now his own boss is underscored by his final claim to "own and operate own typewriter." Read this way, the piece is a kind of ironic Horatio Alger story, a story of success based not on working hard and seizing opportunity but on escaping real work by becoming a novelist. Faulkner is making fun of himself and his artistic ambitions. Once we notice the ironic distance opened up between the narrator and the protagonist of this abbreviated story, however, we realize that the narrator represents a *persona* quite distinct from that of his bumbling character. Indeed, the narrator is using this character partly to mask, and partly to reveal, himself. He is a cryptic ironist displaying his wit while eluding our efforts to pin him down. If we focus on the behavior of this figure, the storyteller, we begin to gain a perspective on Faulkner himself that is inaccessible to us from a simply corrected version. We need the facts, of course, but we need them less to correct the story than to interpret it, to see what it reveals as well as what it is hiding.

The storyteller makes his character the butt of an ongoing joke, as we've seen. But he is not without mercy. Indeed, he takes a bemused attitude toward his protagonist, both exposing and protecting him as he rolls along. In the postmaster story, the narrator seems insistent that Faulkner was not fired from his job as postmaster. He doesn't deny the claim that he threw "all incoming mail in the garbage," but notes that how he "disposed of outgoing mail" was "never proved." (How could it be?) The inspectors were thus "foiled." They couldn't nail him after all, and thus "by mutual agreement" (between themselves or between them and Faulkner?), he was allowed to resign. In an ostensible effort to protect his disgraced protagonist, the narrator exposes the probable firing he is so obviously covering up. Now in fact, Faulkner was not fired from the postmaster job, although he clearly deserved to be. In the course of his nearly three years as postmaster, he became infamous for failing to deal responsibly with either the outgoing or the incoming mail. He opened and closed the post office at his own whim, discarded what he saw as junk mail, read incoming journals that interested him before slotting them into post office boxes, and used the back room for poker with his friends. Finally complaints reached the U.S. Post Office, which sent an inspector to investigate. Not because he was "foiled" but out of respect for his family's prominence in Oxford, the inspector allowed him to resign. In a much quoted line, Faulkner remarked, "You know, all my life I probably will be at the beck and call of somebody who's got money, but never again will I be at the beck and call of every son-of-a-bitch who's got two cents for a stamp."[2] Faulkner, then, is after all partly telling the truth when he says he resigned rather than being fired. He virtually admits that he had failed to do his job, at least with the "incoming mail." But the story doesn't sound at all like the truth. It sounds like he is covering up being fired by distracting us with an ostentatiously tall tale of how he outwitted the post office inspectors. (He even cleared $700, it seems.) The bits and pieces of truth never cohere but are effectively swallowed up in the tall tale. We know we're being lied to. We've known that since the opening sentence, "Born male and single at early age in Mississippi." What we don't know is where, if anywhere, the truth lies. The storyteller is not only having fun with his protagonist as well as his reader, he's also begging the entire question of what may be true, what not, mocking the very promise of the biographical profile he is using.

Faulkner the writer was actually a fairly scrupulous worker; when he went to Hollywood, for example, he wrote reams of prose, believing that he should deliver something in exchange for being paid, even though it turned out that most of it proved useless for filmmaking. So we can surmise that he felt some shame about his postmaster performance and thus perhaps found it a minor relief to confess his sins while submerging them within his tall tale. Of far more importance to him was his alleged participation in World War I. Accordingly, the story he tells about his role in the war provides a more dramatic example of the storyteller's strategy of evasion and revelation. "War came. Liked British uniform," he begins this episode of his life. Again, he tells an extravagant story that simultaneously hides and reveals.

The facts, in brief and so far as they are knowable, are these. When the United States entered the war, Faulkner began to consider signing up, but he wanted a commission. In particular, he wanted one in the Air Force, saturated as his imagination was with stories of flying aces whose exploits he followed even before the war began. He told his family that he had applied for a position in the American Air Force but was turned away for being too short and frail. Meanwhile, Estelle Oldham, the love of his life, became engaged to another man, and his desire to get away from Oxford grew urgent. He went to visit his friend Phil Stone in New Haven, Connecticut, and there they conspired—with the aid of a group of British students and ex-soldiers—to pass themselves off as British so as to join the Canadian military. Stone eventually took a different path, but Faulkner persisted. Claiming to be a British citizen, with forged papers to show that he had been born in the county of Middlesex and a forged letter from one Reverend Mr. Edward Twimberly-Thorndyke testifying to his credentials as an upstanding young Englishman, Faulkner presented himself at the British recruiting office in New York City. As David Minter aptly puts it in his biography of Faulkner, "Whether bemused, fooled, or desperate for recruits, England's representatives accepted her adoptive son" (Minter, 31). In short, the ruse worked, at least insofar as it enabled Faulkner to enter Canadian RAF training near Toronto on July 9, 1918. By all accounts he proved an avid and capable cadet, but the war ended before he could complete his training. Indeed, as far as the records show, he never reached the stage of actually flying a plane. Yet upon his return to Oxford in November 1918, he wore the uniform of the RFC (the more prestigious British corps), walked with a limp and a cane, and claimed he had suffered an injury being shot down over France that had required the insertion of a steel plate in his head. His British mask had worked, so why not adopt the injured veteran's mask? It is noteworthy that he now used the name Faulkner rather than Falkner, having added the "u" on the same fraudulent forms he submitted when he joined the RAF.

Faulkner was eventually to put aside the uniform and give up on the limp (which some said he occasionally forgot to perform), finding other poses to assume—the poet, the dandy, the bohemian, for example—but he never entirely quit telling the story of his plane crash, although it varied considerably. In his biography of Faulkner, Joseph Blotner rehearses some of the more hilarious versions. My personal favorite is the one in which Faulkner claimed to have fallen "uninjured through a thatched roof and land [ed] . . . in the soup tureen of a peasant family's Sunday dinner."[3] The version he offers up in his 1930 *Forum* profile, however, is more telling.

Here, Faulkner says that he flew planes in the war as a pilot but doesn't explicitly insist that he got to France, although he certainly implies that he crashed under wartime circumstances. That assumed, he tells another tall tale. The protagonist here has no real desire to fight for Wilsonian principles, he just likes the uniform, and the British one at that. He proves a disaster as a pilot, twice crashing his plane. He is a shallow, vainglorious, and incompetent buffoon. Little wonder that the British are glad to see him go; when he says "well done," the king is expressing relief at his departure, not gratitude for his service. But here again, even as he is poking fun at his protagonist, the storyteller is at once revealing and obscuring the truth. The plane crash story is blown up and punctured at the same time; he crashed not just once, but twice, but then what matters is the cost of the planes. The planes are worth £2,000 apiece, compared with Faulkner, whose departure costs the British government only $83.40. The war itself is reduced to a matter of money. The young man who went off to Canada for training in the summer of 1918, full of enthusiasm for his anticipated glory has now and long since recognized the decisive gap between dreams of heroism and the experience of war, a theme on which he will write some of his greatest fiction. The account he gives here of the war has in its way just as sharp a critical edge as Hemingway's in *In Our Time*.

But unlike Hemingway, Faulkner missed the war, and he is inadvertently admitting it here. He makes, after all, no claim to aerial combat. His planes crashed, but there is no account of him as the pilot in France surviving the crashes. It is as if he weren't there. And of course, he wasn't. He is distancing himself from his own lies about what he did in the war, but renewing them at the same time. Indeed he knew he had lied, but he couldn't give up on the story, since for him the story had become in some fundamental sense, true. How did this come about?

When Faulkner came home to Oxford decked out in the uniform of an RFC Lieutenant, he was in one sense masking his failures and losses. He had not been to France, he had not fought in combat, he had not married Estelle, and although he had been writing poetry for years now, he had published nothing. In his uniform he commanded a certain respect, at least for a while. His tales of battle also drew attention and admiration. He had, after all, always told a good story, and he had real whoppers to tell now. It was quite a performance while it lasted. His imagination had been so engaged by the stories he heard from and about soldiers, as well as by his own training— learning airplanes, war tactics, and military discipline—that the tales he told about his experiences essentially became his experiences. Faulkner's first piece of published fiction, "Landing in Luck," appeared in the University of Mississippi campus newspaper the following year. It tells the story of a young cadet in training whose close call with a fatal landing echoes many of the stories Faulkner told about his own training flights in Canada.[4] In one sense, Faulkner is relying on autobiography for his material, as do many young writers, but in another sense he has already projected on the screen of his memory an alternative and imagined autobiography. What he actually "did in the war," in other words, is increasingly irrecuperable, replaced by the memories he has sustained and embellished in telling and re-telling his war stories. "Landing in Luck" however er enables him to step back from and ironize his tall tales, in this instance to reveal his protagonist as a terrified and incompetent pilot, who is nonetheless ready to take credit for his sheer luck. Young Thompson basks in the reputation he acquires as a result of his miraculously "lucky" landing. As in the 1930 profile, adopting the stance of the storyteller provides Faulkner with a kind of amnesty from the charges of failure that haunted him, a temporary immunity that allows him to speak freely, indeed to tell the truth. As we shall see, adopting the storyteller's persona would eventually prove crucial to Faulkner's practice as a novelist, enabling him to hide himself far more successfully than he does in "Landing in Luck" while elaborating fictions through which his imagination could break down and reinvent narrative form itself.

"Landing in Luck" appeared in *The Mississippian*, the local university paper, in 1919. Faulkner did not return to serious prose writing until January 1925, when he arrived in New Orleans and began his first novel, *Soldier's Pay*, initially titled "Mayday," which was published in 1926. A dark portrait of the return home of a wounded war veteran, the novel is based on Faulkner's experiences with and among soldiers and cadets in Toronto. It is as if his memories, and the changes wrought on them by his imagination, had been put on hold for seven years. *Soldier's Pay* is not a great novel, but it is a moving one, and it served to usher Faulkner into his long delayed vocation as a novelist. The question is why the delay? The short answer is that he was writing poetry, largely bad poetry. A fuller answer requires us to follow some of the other stories told about and by Faulkner.

From the time he was nine years old, William Faulkner would respond to the perennially annoying adult question, "What do you want to be when you grow up?" by saying "I want to be a writer like my great-granddaddy" (Blotner, 23). There is a certain irony implicit in this no doubt pleasing espousal of a strong family tie and a gentlemanly profession. For although Faulkner's great-grandfather had indeed written several books, one of which had even sold well, his large and resonant reputation was by no means primarily that of a writer. A self-made man, civil war colonel, and gilded age railroad magnate, William Clarke Falkner led an active, controversial, and regularly violent life. He was, in fact, shot dead by his erstwhile business partner, on the main street of Ripley, Mississippi, eight years before his great-grandson and namesake William Cuthbert Faulkner was born in 1897. As Faulkner was to remark many years after being nine, "People at Ripley talk of him as if he were still alive, up in the hills someplace, and might come in at any time."[5] William Clarke Falkner was to become the source and model of several major figures in Faulkner's fiction, but his great-grandson's identification with him as a "writer" is both disingenuous and revealing.

At nine, William Faulkner was already straddling the contradiction in his nature between the aspiring artist and the muscular man of action his great-grandfather had actually been. By identifying with him as a "writer," Faulkner could perhaps hold onto both ideals. As he neared adolescence, it became harder. The conflict grew deeper and manifested itself more dramatically as a struggle between Faulkner's creative drive and his need to establish his masculine credentials. There was something feminine about being an artist, as his family and his culture had always taught him. He had learned to draw early, nurtured in this as in all his artistic aspirations by his mother, who was herself a fine watercolorist. It was she who had encouraged his reading and applauded his efforts to write poetry. His father, by contrast, never understood his son's interest in art and literature. Faulkner's immediate family composed itself into a structure that fostered in him an internal conflict of outsized proportions.

Faulkner was the oldest of the four boys born to Murry C. Falkner and his wife, the former Leila Butler Swift. The first three arrived in relatively quick succession: William Cuthbert Falkner, called Billy, on September 25, 1897; Murry Charles Falkner, called Jack, on June 26, 1899; and John Wesley Thompson Falkner III, called Johncy, on September 24, 1901. The fourth, Dean Swift Falkner was born on August 15, 1907, almost six years after Johncy. These data reflect a good deal about the family in which Faulkner grew up. First, the six-year gap between the third and fourth sons reflects a feature of Maud and Murry's marriage that was well recognized by their neighbors and kin; they were not a happy couple. Although Dean became the darling of the family, it is improbable that he was planned. Faulkner certainly knew that his mother was not fond of his father. On her deathbed, Maud would ask her son Billy whether he thought she would have to encounter her husband in heaven. When he said "No, not if you don't want to," she replied, "That's good. I never did like him."[6] Faulkner followed suit. His father was for him a strange and alien figure from early on, a man who neither understood nor supported his wife's relentless pursuit of an education for her sons. Although respected as a Falkner, Murry was not a success in Oxford. His first love was his grandfather's railroad, and when his father J.W.T. Falkner sold it and thereby eliminated his chances of rising to the head of it, he never fully recovered a sense of purpose. He made a living, first in a livery stable and finally as treasurer of the University of Mississippi, largely thanks to the influence of his father. (At one point Murry tried to persuade his wife to move to Texas, where he could become a cowboy. Maud declined the proposal.)

Faulkner's primary bond was with his mother. For one thing, he was her first child—always a fateful position for a boy, especially for one whose father soon aligned himself with his younger brothers. Also, Billy was the only son who physically favored his mother rather than his father, and the only one not to grow up tall, as his father, and the Falkner men in general, had. (Faulkner's full-grown height was just under 5 ft. 6 in.) To use Freudian shorthand, Faulkner's particular Oedipal project was markedly exacerbated by the strength of his bond with his mother and the distance separating them both from his father, not to mention his father's career failures. Little wonder that Faulkner cast his mythically enlarged great-grandfather in the role of the father. His own father posed little threat to his primacy as his mother's favorite, but of course his father also provided no ideal model, either to emulate or to fight. That Faulkner himself came to understand his father in this light is suggested by a story he later told about him. Sitting on the front porch with him after dinner one night, his father tried to open a line of communication with his now grown son by remarking that he'd heard that Faulkner had begun to smoke. Faulkner assented, having taken up pipe smoking. His father offered him a cigar, which Faulkner accepted, and then broke in half. He put one half in his pocket and stuffed his pipe with the other half. His father never offered him tobacco again, as he liked to say in concluding this story (Blotner, 52).

While Murry Falkner was a figure of weakness in his first son's eyes, his wife Maud was the opposite. On her kitchen wall hung a sign saying "Never explain. Never complain" (a Victorian maxim traceable to the British prime minister, Benjamin Disraeli).[7] However disappointed she was in her husband and her marriage, she was determined to raise her sons according to her own lights, her oldest son in particular. For example, having observed that Billy was not going to be as tall as her younger boys, Maud bought him a kind of corset (a canvas vest that laced up in the back and held the shoulders back) at age thirteen and forced him to wear it for almost two years so that he would stand as straight and upright as possible, as his great-grandfather was reputed to have done. (She apparently succeeded; many would notice Faulker's markedly erect posture throughout his life) (Minter, 15; Blotner, 140). Faulkner neither explained nor complained, apparently, even though the brace precluded his playing baseball, among other athletic endeavors he enjoyed. In this story, it is hard to decide what is more disturbing—a mother intent upon squeezing her son upright or a son willing to be so constricted. His cousin, Sally Murry, a partial model for the adventurous little girl Caddy Compson, was similarly cursed at this time, but she so despised the corset that she got her friends to untie it. Although he dutifully wore the corset, Faulkner began to rebel in other ways. He would skip school frequently, wandering in the woods and reading instead. He was known for sitting for hours sometimes in front of his grandfather's bank, just watching and listening to people. He was, in short, withdrawing into himself, silently rebelling against the restrictions imposed by his mother and his small town life, but meanwhile nourishing an intense meditative engagement with poetry. After discarding the corset, he would return to sports, eventually quarterbacking his high school football team, but by then he had split his interior life off from his social one. This split would become fixed in his life for years to come, indeed stalemating his identity within a paralyzing duality. In public he would act out masculine roles, as athlete, prankster, hard drinker. In private, he was caught up in romantic fantasy, lyric excess, and dark dreams of self-destruction. This private self found expression in poetry and a sustaining validation in two key friendships.

The first and more important friendship was with Estelle Oldham, a childhood sweetheart who had grown into a popular and beautiful teenager. More than a year older than Faulkner, Estelle became the center of a hive of attentive suitors from early adolescence. Yet she and Faulkner remained close, even when she went out with others. He could talk to her about poetry and ideas and she responded with interest and understanding. Theirs was a romantic bond, but something else as well—a shared imaginative life. He wrote poetry for her, as well as recited it to her. David Minter, who has provided the most telling account of this relationship, describes Faulkner's "deepest sense of his relationship to Estelle" as "a highly romantic version of a great and star-crossed yet compelling love" (Minter, 28). When Estelle began to receive serious proposals, the relationship entered crisis. Her family refused Faulkner's candidacy as a husband, on the quite reasonable grounds that he had no income and no prospects, unlike the man they preferred, Cornell Franklin, who had a law degree from the University of Mississippi, or "Ole Miss," as it was called, and a good job in Honolulu. Franklin had courted Estelle while in college and exacted her promise to marry him. She had not really felt committed to him, she was to claim, but she nevertheless married him on April 18, 1918. Her story bears an uncanny resemblance to the story of Daisy Buchanan in F. Scott Fitzgerald's *The Great Gatsby*. Daisy is in love with Gatsby, but he has no money or future. She marries Tom Buchanan even though she doesn't love him. The night before the wedding, she is in tears for hours, insisting that she can't marry Tom because she is in love with Gatsby. She loses the string of pearls Tom has given her as a wedding gift. On the night before her wedding, Estelle is up all night in tears, so hysterical that her aunt offers to call the wedding off. Estelle has lost her engagement ring. In both cases, the jewelry is found and the wedding goes forward, despite the bride's condition, but also because she refuses to back out.

It is difficult to overestimate the impact of this loss on Faulkner's fragile identity. His "world went to pieces," as his brother would later put it (Blotner, 56). His immediate recourse was the other friend with whom he shared some of his private thoughts, Phil Stone. Faulkner left Oxford on March 30, 1918, for New Haven, where his friend and mentor Phil Stone was finishing his Yale law degree. Stone had for several years been reading Faulkner's poetry and encouraging his creative efforts. With two B.A.'s, one from Ole Miss and one from Yale, Stone saw himself as a crucial intellectual resource for Faulkner, providing him with the latest modernist poetry and spending long hours talking literature with him. Stone was to serve as one source for the lawyer Gavin Stevens, a character in the Snopes novels who loves to talk abstractly and at length. But he was never fully to reconcile himself to the fact that he had not wholly created Faulkner as an artist. Which is not to say that he wasn't an important influence. And during these years, he was especially useful as someone who recognized Faulkner's talent. Except for Estelle and to a degree, his mother, Phil Stone was the only person in Oxford who did, and Stone's education gave him both the literary sophistication and the social authority to make that recognition significant. Stone invited Faulkner to join him in New Haven so as to withdraw and recuperate from the crisis generated by Estelle's impending wedding. And, as we have seen, it was Stone who conspired with and assisted Faulkner in his campaign to join the RAF, making the needed social connections and sharing with him an informal course in how to sound like an upper-class Englishman.

Upon Faulkner's return from Canada, Stone and he resumed their friendship. Stone again encouraged Faulkner's poetic endeavors and eventually helped to get his first volume of poetry, *The Marble Faun*, published in 1924. Stone's interest played its part in Faulkner's persisting loyalty to poetry, but what primarily stimulated Faulkner's poetic output was Estelle, who began to come home for family visits in June 1919. She arrived with her first child Victoria, nicknamed "Cho-Cho," and stayed through September, and thus was present when Faulkner's first published poem, "L'Apres-Midi d'un Faune," appeared in *The New Republic* in August, 1919. Estelle would return, eventually with Cho-Cho and her son Malcolm, several times in the course of the 1920s, but almost always without her husband. As her marriage gradually broke apart, she saw a lot of Faulkner, who continued writing poetry primarily for her, but also in the hope of publishing again. During these years he did publish his work in *The Mississippian*, but he never again found a national audience for his poetry. In retrospect, it is not hard to see why.

Here is part VIII of *Vision in Spring*, a poetic sequence that Faulkner bound and presented to Estelle in 1921:

> Pierrot, sitting chill on a wall in darkness,
> Feeling the sharp cold stone stinging his palms,
> Seeing the darkness freeze from roof to roof
>   between the houses;—
> Stirs, and clasps his arms.
> Stars swing back across the empty street,
> And ghostly faces are blown like stars across his heart.
>
> Now that the city grows black and chill and empty,—
> Who am I, thinks Pierrot, who am I
> To stretch my soul out rigid across the sky?[8]

The echo of Eliot's "The Love Song of J. Alfred Prufrock" is unmistakable. Faulkner has immersed himself in French symbolist poetry, as well as in T. S. Eliot, A. E. Housman, Conrad Aiken, and other contemporary poets. He is trapped by the poetic structures that he's been studying so carefully. He is also trapped by the aestheticism of late nineteenth-century decadents. His *persona*, Pierrot, like his counterpart in the earlier "The Marble Faun," remains paralyzed, doomed to passive observation and active dreaming. As the faun puts it,

> Why am I sad? I?
> Why am I not content? The sky

Warms me and yet I cannot break
My marble bonds.[9]

Faulkner is struggling to articulate his deepest feelings, of longing and despair, of potential rapture and anticipated death, but he is bound tightly within the limitations of poetic form itself. The result is a self-portrait composed of heavily derivative language and constrained within an obsessively narcissistic focus. Although often erotic, his poems always portray the Pierrot figure as frozen, unable to join the world of the sexually alive. What power they have comes from the sense of lyrical excess they are designed to repress.

In the fall of 1919, Faulkner signed up for some courses at the university, but proved interested only in studying French. (He made a "D" in English.) He published some poems and reviews in the campus journals and drawings in the campus yearbook, but otherwise he was not deeply engaged with college life. Much as he had stayed on one extra fall in order to play football in high school, he now stayed on at college primarily to publish his work and to work with a theatrically oriented group of students for whom he wrote a verse play, "Marionnettes." Interestingly, he agreed to join a fraternity, SAE, but only because his father and grandfather had been members. He was still straddling the gap between the masculine world of his paternal lineage and the feminizing world of art. And a significant part of his male identification was fueled by drinking to excess, a habit for which he gained a reputation during these years, particularly in Clarksdale and Memphis, where he would go, often with Phil Stone, to escape Oxford. The two built friendships with various poker players, liquor smugglers, and prostitutes, providing Faulkner with both rich material for his later fiction and the opportunity to enact a masculinity still very much under threat. By the fall of 1920, Faulkner had abandoned his brief career as a student and was spending more and more time on such excursions; sometimes he would simply disappear alone, no one knowing where he'd gone. Back in town, now largely out of uniform, he often dressed like a dandy. Because of his apparent arrogance and his largely jobless state, he was known first as "the Count," and then as "Count No' Count." In private, Faulkner was still reading widely, writing his carefully wrought but self-absorbed poetry, and wrung with failure and self-doubt; but publicly, he seemed to take himself a good deal more seriously than most people in Oxford thought he deserved.

His friends were worried about him. When his fellow Oxford writer Stark Young invited him to come to New York City for a while, and when Phil Stone encouraged the idea, Faulkner accepted. He spent part of the fall of 1921 revisiting New Haven and the rest working in a bookstore in New York and living in Greenwich Village. He wrote a couple of short stories, and at least one poem, "Two Puppets in a Fifth Avenue Window," (Blotner, 107) but it was clear to his family that he was drifting. Phil Stone once again came to the rescue, arranging for Faulkner to be appointed postmaster of the university substation in Oxford. Although Faulkner adamantly refused the offer twice, he finally agreed, reluctantly returning to take up his new position in December 1921.

As we have seen, Faulkner's three-year tenure as a postmaster was not a success, but it proved advantageous to him in two ways. He drew a salary of $1,500.00 per year so he didn't have to find odd jobs in order to live, and he spent much of his time in the post office writing, as many customers would complain after failing to distract him in order to get their mail. Although it would seem improbable, he also became a scoutmaster during these years, taking the town's boys out for camping trips on which he would teach them woodcraft and tell them ghost stories around the campfire. But not so improbable after all, because Faulkner was always open to children in ways he never could be with their elders. Beneath his various poses, he was a deeply shy person. So he was actually good at this job, one that afforded him a space for relaxation as well as masculine bonding. But his sojourn as leader of the Boy Scouts was cut short when the townspeople decided he was drinking too heavily to be a scoutmaster. Meanwhile he found other ways to reinforce his masculine identity, whether by spreading rumors of an illegitimate child or by mastering the game of golf in the local "golf pasture" (Minter, 47). His artistic career, however, seemed blocked. He continued to find a publishing venue only in the local campus paper, except for the publication, prophetically enough as we shall see, of one of the poems from "Vision in Spring" in the June 1922 issue of *The Double Dealer*, a New Orleans literary journal (Blotner, 113). Without abandoning poetry, however, he was beginning to turn toward prose. In *The Mississippian,* he published several pieces of literary criticism as well as a short, plotless sketch, "The Hill," in which his lyric excess is at least partly channeled through a character, nameless though he remains.[10] And according to his brother John, Faulkner was sending pieces to magazines, pieces most likely to have been fiction. Once upon receiving the usual rejection, he announced to his mother,

"This one is back from the *Saturday Evening Post*, but the day will come when they'll be glad to buy anything I write, and these too, without changing a word" (Blotner, I, 378). Once freed from the post office job in late 1924, Faulkner grew increasingly restless, planning a trip to Europe as soon as *The Marble Faun* was published. As the publication process dragged on, a friend suggested to Faulkner that he take a trip to New Orleans. Thus it was that he met Sherwood Anderson for the first time. Anderson was married to Elizabeth Prall, the woman who had hired and worked with Faulkner in the New York bookshop. Although shy and disinclined to take advantage of his friendship with Elizabeth, in October Faulkner finally showed up at the Anderson apartment on Jackson Square, the heart of the Vieux Carre. It is not clear how long Faulkner spent in New Orleans, but it is clear that he and Anderson immediately hit it off. Faulkner was a deep admirer of Anderson's work and found the man in person thoroughly engaging. They spent evenings walking around the Vieux Carre, talking literature and life, drinking, and on at least one occasion visiting a former madam. Anderson apparently wrote up the story of this incident within a matter of days. "A Meeting South," which depicts "a little Southern man," a wounded soldier, telling his story to a retired prostitute, arrived at his publisher's address in New York on November 12 (Blotner, 123). When he left town, some time in late October, Faulkner had a standing invitation at the Andersons'.

Faulkner finally received his copy of *The Marble Faun* on December 19. Phil Stone had written a preface and was manically pushing the book both locally and beyond. Against the backdrop of Stone's almost madcap publicity drive, Faulkner appears rather cool and calm. Pleased with the book's publication, he nonetheless understood it for what it was—work long since done. Staying through the Christmas holidays, in part to spend time with Estelle and her children who were again home for a visit, Faulkner left town as soon as he could, ostensibly for Europe.

Arriving in New Orleans in January 1925, Faulkner may not himself have been surprised when he quickly decided to stay on for a while rather than find an outward bound ship. Sherwood Anderson was out of town, not to return for two months, but his wife Elizabeth welcomed Faulkner enthusiastically, putting him up until March when he found an apartment of his own. Like Anderson and his wife, Faulkner found New Orleans a congenial city, not least because it harbored a colony of active and convivial artists and writers, many of them centered around the journal, *The Double Dealer*. For the first time, Faulkner was living among people whose interests and ambitions he shared. Playing the wounded soldier again, as well as the Bohemian poet, he found a responsive audience for his war stories and a sophisticated appreciation for his talent. And of course, unlike Oxford, New Orleans believed in pleasure. Although he was planning another volume of poetry, he almost immediately began writing and publishing sketches for both *The Double Dealer* and the *New Orleans Times-Picayune*. And by late February, he had begun a novel which he completed by the middle of May. How do we account for this fateful change of direction?

In retrospect, of course, it might seem more appropriate to ask why he devoted so many years to poetry than why he took up fiction as he approached his twenty-eighth birthday. But that approach would not do justice to the seriousness of Faulkner's poetic project. Poetry was for the young Faulkner both a discipline and a calling, representing the purest form of art. Years later he told Jean Stein, "I am a failed poet. Maybe every novelist wants to write poetry first, finds he can't, and then tries the short story, which is the next most demanding form after poetry. And, failing at that, only then does he take up novel writing."[11] Speaking as a Nobel Laureate for fiction, Faulkner may perhaps be accused of false modesty. But in fact, his is more a confession, since "finds he can't" is the pivot on which this particular tale turns. Faulkner never changed his conviction that as an art form, poetry was superior to narrative. What he had begun to realize even before meeting Anderson was that he would never achieve the order of success to which he aspired if he kept on writing poetry. Faulkner was more fundamentally devoted to success than he was to poetry. And he was well aware of it. Once when he and Phil Stone were talking, Stone criticized Amy Lowell and her cohort by saying that "they always had one eye on the ball and the other on the grandstand." Faulkner replied that his "personal trouble as a poet seemed to be that he had one eye on the ball and the other eye on Babe Ruth" (Blotner, 71). Behind his various masks and beneath his layers of self-doubt, Faulkner saw himself not just as a writer, but a great writer. What he lacked, and what his poetry had proven unable to command, was recognition. Phil Stone had recognized his gifts but saw him first and last as a poet. What Sherwood Anderson recognized was a storyteller. "You've got too much talent," he told Faulkner. "You can do it too easy, in too many different ways. If you're not careful, you'll never write anything" (Blotner, 135).

What in part prompted this remark on Anderson's part was the story of Al Jackson. On their afternoon walks and over their evening drinks in New Orleans, Faulkner and Anderson had begun to make up this story together, eventually sending each other letters in which each took the story further, invented more characters, enriching the fable through dialogue. Al Jackson, as Faulkner later summed him up, was "a descendant of Andrew Jackson, left in [a]...Louisiana swamp after the battle of Chalmette, no longer half-horse half-alligator, but now half-man half-sheep and presently half-shark" (Blotner, 134). Sharing an understanding of southwestern humor, Anderson and Faulkner competed to see who could make more outlandish the story of the Jackson family and their gradual regression from man to fish. Although neither won the game, Faulkner realized he could play it, and with a worthy opponent. As David Minter aptly puts it, "As a writer, [Anderson] was accomplished enough to be impressive, yet flawed enough not to seem overwhelming—a combination that made him an almost perfect master" (Minter, 51). Anderson's recognition, then, proved critical in regenerating Faulkner's self-confidence as a writer, and their joint production of the Al Jackson stories provided a model he was to use in shaping narratives for years to come—conversation itself. As he apprenticed himself to fiction over the coming years, he frequently framed stories within a two-person dialogue. In *Absalom, Absalom!* he was to structure an entire novel around several key conversations.

With Anderson as model and interlocutor, Faulkner now enjoyed a new experience in his life as a writer: he was actually being read, not to mention being paid for his work.

For the first time, he had readers, both those who subscribed to the local *Times-Picayune* and those of a more intellectual bent who read and supported *The Double Dealer*. Among the authors published in this journal were Hart Crane, Djuna Barnes, Ezra

Pound, Thornton Wilder, Ernest Hemingway, and of course Sherwood Anderson. The magazine's editors were clearly in touch with the current modernist writers both at home and abroad, and the culture they created and inhabited in the Vieux Carre was by no means provincial.

Faulkner went into high gear in this setting. He wrote furiously every day, producing prose with a steady intensity he had never achieved as a poet. Between January and September 1925, some twenty prose pieces of his appeared in the two New Orleans publications. Having an audience he could imagine himself addressing without fear of ridicule, he entered into an imaginary conversation with a real community. Further, the prose sketches he produced began to enable him to write about something besides himself. Engaged in describing various New Orleans "characters," he began to imagine dialogues with them. Gradually they began to have dialogues with each other, as in "The Liar," a story that depicts the kind of storefront tale swapping Faulkner would later exploit so brilliantly in *The Hamlet*.[12] Most important, Faulkner could remain hidden, protected by the storyteller's *persona* he was learning to adopt. The "I" of his lyric poetry began to be displaced by newly discovered voices through which he could speak more freely, voices that no longer sounded like Prufrock. As he moved on with his prose experiments that spring, Faulkner returned to his war "experience" as the basis for his first novel, *Soldier's Pay*. The stories he had told about himself, he now translated into a fictional world where Julian Lowe is a returning cadet who looks upon the world "with a yellow and disgruntled eye" because "they had stopped the war on him."[13] But if Lowe to some degree represents Faulkner, he is nevertheless distinct from another character, Donald Mahon, who also resembles Faulkner. An officer who has returned from the battlefront maimed and terminally wounded in both mind and spirit, Mahon enacts the role of the wounded airman Faulkner had made up for himself. Splitting and doubling himself into these two figures, Faulkner stands back to watch. In short, narrative prose was facilitating distance, and a certain safety, allowing his imagination to roam more freely and without threat of exposure even as he explored his darkest fears.

But William Faulkner, novelist, by no means sprang full blown into life that spring. In a piece published in *The Double Dealer* for April 1925, "Verse Old and Nascent: A Pilgrimage," Faulkner ostentatiously bids farewell to poetry, attributing his adolescent interest in poetry first to "the purpose of furthering various philanderings in which I was engaged," and "secondly, to complete a youthful gesture I was then making of being 'different' in a small town" (*EPP*, 115). Once sidetracked by the seductions of Swinburne, he has now recovered his literary senses, turning to the tradition of Shakespeare, Spenser, the Elizabethans, Keats, and Shelley, finding there "the spiritual beauty which the moderns strive vainly for with trickery, and yet beneath it one knows are entrails; masculinity" (*EPP*, 117). But even as he distances himself from his poetic past, he remains devoted to the ideal of poetry, hoping for a "Keats in embryo, . . . someone who can write something beautiful and passionate and sad instead of saddening" (*EPP*, 118). And in the same issue of the magazine, he publishes a poem, "The Faun," another version of the faun as the figure of the desiring male whose "panting puzzled heart is wrung and blind" (*EPP*, 119). Even as he posed as a cynic looking back with pity on his youthful amours, Faulkner was in fact still writing poetry for a woman. At least this time it was a different one.

In New Orleans, Faulkner had met Helen Baird, a young woman slight of form like Estelle, but more worldly, skeptical, and rambunctious of spirit. In the early summer of 1925, he spent his time with Helen on the beach in Pascagoula, Mississippi, even though Estelle was still in Oxford and already considering a divorce. Over the course of the next year, Faulkner pursued and fell in love with Helen, and, true to form, began writing poems for her. Just as he had hand lettered and hand bound "Vision in Spring" for Estelle, he would hand letter and hand bind a little volume of sonnets called "Helen: A Courtship." In January 1926, he presented her with another handmade book, "Mayday." This one, notably, was a medieval allegory about the knight, Sir Galwyn of Arthgyl, who is on a vain romantic quest that ends in his death. Faulkner proposed marriage to Helen, but she turned him down. Although she was fond of him as an eccentric bohemian and shared his interest in literature, Helen did not take him seriously as a suitor. She would later advise a friend against reading *Mosquitoes*, the novel Faulkner dedicated to her, calling it "no good" (Minter, 60). In 1927 she married a lawyer. Again thwarted in love, Faulkner again wrote poems about his unfulfilled desires, offering them in tribute to a woman who had rejected him. But at the same time he played out the familiar role of failed lover, he was gaining distance on that performance, indeed on all his masks and poses, in his fiction.

In *Mosquitoes* (1927), the novel he tentatively began while in Europe and took up seriously in June 1926, the character Dawson Fairchild—a novelist based largely on Sherwood

Anderson—remarks that a writer is "always writing it for some woman, that he fondly believes he's stealing a march on some brute bigger or richer or handsomer than he is; I believe that every word a writing man writes is put down with the ultimate intention of impressing some woman that probably don't care anything at all for literature, as is the nature of women" (Blotner, I, 512). In "Verse Old and Nascent," Faulkner had made fun of the young poet who sought to woo his love with poetry. Now he gives the idea full expression, laying it out for scrutiny even as he disavows responsibility for it. Dawson Fairchild is a loveable windbag, on occasion capable of genuine insight but also liable to contradict himself repeatedly as he talks on and on about art, women, the limits of formal education, and the deficiencies of modern youth. Faulkner makes him a mouthpiece for a variety of speculations, especially as here about the artist's primary drives. At another point in one of Fairchild's breathless mono- logues, he tries to find terms for explaining what he calls the writer's "perversion":

> There is a kind of spider or something. The female is the larger, and when the male goes to her he goes to death: she devours him during the act of conception. And that's man: a kind of voraciousness that makes an artist stand beside himself with a notebook in his hand always, putting down all the charming things that ever happen to him, killing them for the sake of some problematical something he might or might never use.[14]

Because Fairchild has been identified early as capable of wild ideas as well as tall tales, he can say pretty much anything he wants. As character, he is endowed with a freedom to speak with an imaginative largesse that Faulkner as narrator cannot indulge if he is to be credible. So he sets up the narrator as a kind of listener, following Conrad's example if not yet nearing his achievement. By relocating his anxieties about art from a threatened and defensive "I" to a garrulous and uncensored "he," Faulkner releases his imagination from its moorings in self-absorption, enabling it to spew forth all sorts of confused and contradictory notions that had been pent up.

As he worked at his new trade of fiction, Faulkner found that it unleashed his observations as well as his experiences, making more of both directly accessible to his imagination. He came to see that he had always been standing "beside himself," taking down notes in a mental "notebook" just as he had always sketched things as he walked around town or in the woods. (Like many novelists, Faulkner had a prodigious memory. He could, for example, recite virtually any passage from Shakespeare and the Bible on demand.) But he also struggled with his new stance, as the Dawson Fairchild passage reveals. The artist may have magical powers, but he is alienated from life, and potentially dangerous to himself and others. Furthermore, Faulkner had to learn how to write fiction that would live up to his ambitions. Both *Soldier's Pay* and *Mosquitoes* are rich in promise, but neither is an accomplished novel—which is to say that Faulkner was still learning how to control his newly untethered imagination. To that end, he needed to put in some practice at his new trade, but he also needed to get out of his own way and give the one standing "beside himself" his head. His six months in Europe helped him to do both.

Although Phil Stone had written letters of introduction for his young protégé to notable writers such as Joyce and Yeats, Faulkner never used them, no doubt knowing that Stone knew none of them himself. Stone had encouraged Faulkner to go to Europe on the theory that he would be discovered as a poet there, much as Robert Frost had been in England. But Faulkner had a different project in mind. After landing in Genoa, he and his travel companion Bill Spratling went on a walking tour in the Italian countryside for a couple of weeks and then split up. Faulkner headed for Paris, where he would live for the next two and one-half months on the Rue Servandoni, across the street from the Luxembourg Gardens. Although he may have gone once to a restaurant frequented by Joyce in the hope of sighting the great man, Faulkner otherwise kept to himself, never having acquired "the café habit," as he described it to his mother:

(Everyone else in France spends the evening sitting in cafes playing cards or listening to music.) Especially the poets. They sit from 6 to 12 o'clock in rows smoking cigarettes in the cafes, like pigeons on the roof of a barn.[15]

Faulkner continued his now fixed habit of writing in the "forenoon" as he called it, walking around town in the afternoon, and dining frugally in a cheap restaurant in the evening. His bohemian pose was limited to making a pilgrimage to Père Lachaise to visit Oscar Wilde's tomb and to growing a beard. His favorite afternoon pastime was watching the little boys and old men sail their toy sailboats on the pool in the Luxembourg Gardens. But what he mainly did was work on two novels.

One of these he would publish as *Mosquitoes*. The other, called "Elmer," he would never publish. As we have noted, *Mosquitoes* reveals the turmoil of ideas and possibilities opened up by Faulkner's turn to fiction but effectively objectifies them in characters who embody various versions of the artist. They are gathered on a boat, cruising around Lake Pontchartrain, mostly talking, mostly about art and sex. Among the minor off-stage characters is one Faulkner, a "funny man" who "said he was a liar by profession and he made good money at it." In Hitchcockian fashion, Faulkner puts in a cameo appearance as a shabbily dressed and sunburned stranger who is "crazy. Not dangerous: just crazy" (*Mosquitoes*, 145). In "Elmer," by contrast, Faulkner tells the story of a young artist, an aspiring painter named Elmer Hodge, but can get no distance on him, no relief from sharing his trials. Even though Elmer is physically Faulkner's opposite—tall and gangly—he is trapped by the same conflicts that had so haunted Faulkner—between art and life, between a woman and his career, between male and female sexual identities. Much is revealed about Elmer's interior struggles, indeed too much. A sign, perhaps, of Faulkner's final frustration with the manuscript is his representation of Elmer using one of his watercolors as toilet paper.[16] He wrote his mother that he had put the *Mosquitoes* manuscript aside because "I dont think I am quite old enough to write it as it should be written—dont know quite enough about people" (Blotner, 162). The problem with "Elmer," by contrast seems to have been that he knew, or was learning, too much about himself, more than he was willing to admit or able to process. What little ironic distance he could summon up proved insufficient either to free or to protect him from the figure he was drawing in Elmer. He would later say that he never published "Elmer" because it was "funny, but not funny enough." In fact, as Joseph Blotner has noted, "there was little that was very funny about Elmer" (Blotner, 165).

Abandoning "Elmer," Faulkner focused his attention on short stories, writing his mother glowing even if mildly ironic accounts of his progress. In late October 1925 he reported, "I'm writing a story now—the best one yet, as usual," and several days later he again bragged, "I have just finished the 4th best short story in the world—the other 3 being the ones I wrote previous to it" (TOH, 200, 202). By this time, Faulkner's novel, *Soldier's Pay*, had been accepted for publication and he was anxious to get home. He planned to sell his short stories and get back to work on *Mosquitoes*. On one front, he succeeded; *Soldier's Pay* was published in February 1926, and *Mosquitoes* appeared in April of 1927. But on the other, he met with steady rejection. Faulkner would not sell a short story until *Forum* accepted "A Rose for Emily" in 1930. In the face of his disappointment, however, he wrote a third novel that he knew was a crucial breakthrough. *Flags in the Dust* called forth the old tales and talking of his youth and suddenly opened wide for him the gates to his own imagined world. As he worked away at it, during the summer of 1927, Faulkner grew genuinely excited. In July he wrote his editor Horace Liveright, "the new novel is coming fine. It is much better than that other stuff. I believe that at last I have learned to control the stuff and fix it on something like rational truth" (*SL*, 37). In October Faulkner sent off the manuscript, writing Liveright, "At last and certainly, as El Orens' sheik said, I have written THE book, of which those other things were but foals. I believe it is the damdest book you'll look at this year, and any other publisher" (*SL*, 38). Ready for a vacation, Faulkner also asked for some advance money, as he was planning "an expedition with a lady friend for purposes of biological research" (Blotner, I, 557). Whoever it was that Faulkner was going to celebrate with—and we've never found out who it was—he was thoroughly exhilarated by his new novel. Why he was so thrilled is not hard to understand. For the first time, Faulkner had populated a novel with figures drawn from his family history and his local environment. The stories he had grown up hearing now made their way into his text through the voices of an "Old Bayard" Sartoris and an Aunt Jenny Du Pre, behind and beyond whom hovers the long dead but ever-present Old Colonel John Sartoris, based on the revered William Clarke Falkner.

The patriarch, John Sartoris, survives the death of his brother Bayard in the civil war, returns to build his railroad, and dies in a duel with his business partner. His great grandson, Bayard survives the death of his brother John in World War I, then comes home to Jefferson in guilt and despair. Meanwhile, a host of subplots proliferate. Another homecoming warrior is Horace Benbow. He's never seen battle, but he has developed an obsession with glassblowing; he brings home an elaborate glassblowing apparatus from Italy. Horace has a sister, Narcissa, with whom he is in love. Narcissa loves him too, but is a cold and proper lady, and so marries Bayard Sartoris. That is, before Bayard manages to kill his grandfather the banker by driving his new car into a ditch and before Bayard manages to kill himself going up in an airplane as untrustworthy as the one his brother John died in over France. Confused yet? But there's more. A smarmy young man named Byron Snopes is writing secret and pornographic letters to Narcissa, who carefully keeps them in her underwear drawer, this against the advice of Bayard's Great-Aunt Jenny, a voice of reason and as well as of humor in the novel. There is also a black family that harbors an ambitious and discontented son who wants to revolt against his parents' loyalty to the Sartoris family. I could go on. The problem is that's exactly what Faulkner did.

We have noticed Faulkner's discovery that fiction allowed him some ironic distance on himself. When he had only one character to work with, as in "Elmer," that distance too easily collapsed. By splitting and doubling himself into two characters, as he did in *Soldier's Pay,* he was able to get sufficient purchase on his experience to represent it. In *Mosquitoes,* by splitting the narrator off as a listener from the characters who speak, he was able to indulge his thoughts without exposing his flank. In *Flags in the Dust,* however, these strategies of splitting and doubling proliferate at a dizzying pace. Characters materialize apace, some out of the thin air of memory, multiplying stories and generating other characters. Little wonder, then, that when Faulkner's friend and agent Ben Wasson tried to edit the manuscript, he complained that there were six novels there. Rather than taking control, as he called it, Faulkner seems rather to have been taken control of—by the onrush of figures and stories now unloosed to wander at will around his imagination. He had discovered his subject, the invented world to which he was to give the name Yoknapatawpha County, but it was too large, too rich, and ultimately too disturbing, to bring into focus yet.

Of course, Faulkner himself didn't see it this way. He was both baffled and severely wounded when Liveright turned the novel down cold. Two years later he described his reaction:

I was shocked: my first emotion was blind protest, then I became objective for an instant, like a parent who is told that its child is a thief or an idiot or a leper; for a dreadful moment I contemplated it with consternation and despair, then like the parent I hid my own eyes in the fury of denial. I clung stubbornly to my illusion. (Blotner, I, 560)

Although he tried to revise the novel, he found that to cut it up and paste it together again was impossible. It was his child, and he "clung" to the "illusion" that it was whole and well. He did allow Ben Wasson to edit it and so the novel was finally published as *Sartoris* in 1928. But meanwhile the ambitious trajectory he had imagined starting with *Flags in the Dust* was blocked.

Just how much was blocked becomes evident when we realize that he had already written several stories in which he had imagined events and characters that were to take him a lifetime to develop fully. "Father Abraham," for example, written sometime late in 1926, just before he turned to "Flags," already constructs the characters of Flem Snopes, Uncle Billy Varner, and the precursor to Ratliff, all of whom would return to life in *The Hamlet* (1940). It also tells the story of the Texas horsetrader, later retold in "Spotted Horses," itself later incorporated into *The Hamlet*. "Evangeline," written in the same period, already tells a version of the story of Charles Bon and Judith Sutpen, later to form the core of *Absalom, Absalom!* (1936). Perhaps even more important, Faulkner had composed, in addition to "Evangeline," three other stories built on the conversation of a reporter named Don and his interlocutor, "I." "Mistral," "Snow," and "The Big Shot," as Estella Schonberg first pointed out, are each early experiments with the dialogue between Quentin and Shreve that occupies the final four chapters of *Absalom, Absalom!*[17] In that novel, where Quentin

Compson splits into two Quentins, and then into Quentin and Shreve, and finally into four figures, Quentin/Henry and Shreve/Charles, the promise of the split and doubled Sartoris brothers would come to fruition. But all of this was put on hold in the fall of 1928.

Still the most incisive account of what happened to and for Faulkner that fall is David Minter's, which goes something like this: Faulkner has apprenticed himself first as a poet, then as a fiction writer, only to find himself a minor regional poet turned a minor regional novelist. He is now thirty years old, and having written three novels, he is reduced to day labor as a painter to make ends meet. Estelle, his childhood sweetheart, has divorced her husband and returned to Oxford with her two children. She awaits the finalization of her divorce and his proposal of marriage. Stuck in a psychological and professional limbo, he continues to write short stories, among them three of particular importance about a group of children named Compson: "A Justice," "When That Evening Sun Go Down," and "Twilight." The last of these would become *The Sound and the Fury*, the result of a treacherous psychological regression that ironically enabled a radical formal innovation. "One day," he said, "I seemed to shut the door between me and all publisher's addresses and book lists. I said to myself, Now I can write." As Minter puts it, "If writing for himself implied freedom to recover more personal materials, writing without concern for publisher's addresses implied freedom to become more experimental" (Minter, 94). The results of this experiment were to stun Faulkner himself. Upon completing it he gave the typescript to Ben Wasson, saying "Read this, Bud. It's a real son of a bitch" (Minter, 105). When he tried to edit the book for publication, Wasson was himself stunned. His efforts to impose clarity through additions and punctuation elicited a blunt response from his friend Faulkner: "Don't make any more additions to the script, bud. I know you mean well, but so do I. I effaced the 2 or 3 you made" (*SL*, 45).

The leap made between *Flags in the Dust* and *The Sound and the Fury*, both published in 1929, remains stunning. If *Flags in the Dust* marked a Balzacian moment, opening up an infinite social and historical array of narrative possibilities, *The Sound and the Fury* marks a Flaubertian moment, revealing a Faulkner who was finding the means for controlling the virtually unlimited resources of language he now discovered were available to him. In a sense, *The Sound and the Fury* is the site of the struggle Faulkner mounts to cope with the flood of imaginative energy released by his turn back into his most private and painful memories. The regression into childhood funds an explosion of passion, which in turn requires an accelerated experimentation with, and mastery over, narrative technique. In *Flags,* Faulkner had basically lined up a disparate set of stories, turning now to one, now to another, and linking them loosely around family tales and the failed heroics of war. Now he found, indeed was forced to find, a means of telling one story, but one that outstripped the limits of the fictional forms he had been using. His imagination now required a new form of narrative. There is no question that the discovery marked by *Flags in the Dust* of his own invented world, "William Faulkner, Sole Owner and Proprietor," was a major one, enabling the Balzacian plenty to come. But it is equally if not more important to recognize that without the formal experimentation displayed in *The Sound and the Fury*, Faulkner's achievement as a novelist would certainly have been different and probably less consequential.

The Sound and the Fury

Although on first reading *The Sound and the Fury* seems far more chaotic than *Flags in the Dust*, it is in fact an exquisitely composed and virtually perfect work. "I worked so hard at that book," Faulkner would later remark, "that I doubt if there's anything in it that didn't belong there" (Minter, 104). Soon after completing it, he told Ben Wasson that he had "worked on it . . . like a poem almost."[18] His favorite and most often repeated account of the novel centered on having "no plan at all," but simply beginning to write, and finding himself caught up in imagining the world of Benjy Compson and his two brothers, and most centrally, a sister named Caddy (*S&F*, 227). He liked to say that he had fallen in love with Caddy, that he "loved her so much that [he] couldn't decide to give her life just for the duration of a short story. She deserved more than that" (*S&F*, 422). Thus he decided to retell the story, first through Quentin's perspective, then through Jason's, and finally, as he sometimes put it, through Faulkner's. Compelling though this love story is, it cannot wholly disguise the fact that Faulkner did indeed develop a plan, that at some point, probably upon completing the first section, he had begun to write with publication squarely in mind. The Benjy section, he realized, could not make sense on its own as a short story. But if it was not to be a short story, what was it to become? Faulkner knew that secreted within it was the larger story of the Compson family itself, and so he sought a way of telling that larger story through further experiments with point of view. This decision led to even more innovative consequences. He may well have begun the Benjy section with no plan and no hope, but by the time he had drafted it he had large plans and even larger hopes.

The opening section of the novel, in fact, is not a story at all, but a pastiche of moments as experienced by Benjy at various points in his life. There is no plot, no beginning or ending. Instead, a dense array of images is established, centered around Benjy's anguished loss of his sister. The principle of composition, then, is more poetic than narrative, and perhaps more pictorial than either, especially if we include cubist painting as a reference point. For through Benjy's consciousness we are shown various scenes and events as if time did not exist. That is, some purely arbitrary sight or word triggers a shift in Benjy's mind from present to past to present, much as a cubist painting moves us from one point of view to another without ever providing a fixed vantage point outside the frame. The effect is a vivid but puzzling sensorium.

Consider the opening page of the novel. The title, "April Seventh, 1928" seems to situate us in a secure chronological time frame, but the scene is at once crisp and dizzying.

Through the fence, between the curling flower spaces, I could see them hitting. They were coming toward where the flag was and I went along the fence. Luster was hunting in the grass by the flower tree. They took the flag out, and they were hitting. Then they put the flag back and they went to the table, and he hit and the other hit. Then they went on, and I went along the fence. Luster came away from the flower tree and we went along the fence and they stopped and we stopped and I looked through the fence while Luster was hunting in the grass.

"Here, caddie." He hit. They went away across the pasture. I held to the fence and watched them going away.

"Listen at you, now." Luster said. "Aint you something, thirty three years old, going on that way. After I done went all the way to town to buy you that cake. Hush up that moaning. Aint you going to help me find that quarter so I can go the show tonight? . . .

We went along the fence and came to the garden fence, where our shadows were. My shadow was higher than Luster's on the fence. We came to the broken place and went through it.

"Wait a minute." Luster said. "You snagged on that nail again. Cant you never crawl through here without snagging on that nail."

Caddy uncaught me and we crawled through. (S&F, 3)

We are instantly thrust into a world of sights and sounds and events, but they are apparently uninflected by any interpretive significance. We are presented with bits and pieces, but it is left up to us how to compose them into some coherent picture. Think of it as a kind of game, a poker game. Let us first bet that the speaker here is a little boy. His speech is simple and linear. Let us be especially clever and say that he is watching a golf game, since people are "hitting" and calling out "caddie." Who Luster is remains uncertain, but we know that he is looking for a lost quarter. Then we become confused. The speaker is not a little boy, but a thirty-three-year-old man who is having his birthday today. If he is taller than Luster, how old is Luster? And what is the still nameless speaker moaning about? We are introduced suddenly to "Caddy," which may help us to line up "caddie" and "Caddy," the homophony that eventually accounts for Benjy's moaning, but meanwhile, where are we?

Snagged by a nail on the fence, Benjy's mind is catapulted back to a memory of Caddy freeing him from the same nail on the same fence. Since this memory is printed in italics, we bet that we're now in a different time frame, one in which, lo and behold, Benjy actually is a little boy. Maybe we're not willing to raise the bet, but we're not yet willing to fold our cards either.

The poker metaphor, I think, helps us to see how central to Faulkner's strategy is his anticipation of the reader's responses to his prose. He invites us to speculate in order to figure out what is happening, responding to our guesses with further bits and pieces of information. Once we learn how to read in this fashion, of course, we are caught up in more than a game. By compelling us to assemble a picture of the world as experienced by Benjy, Faulkner teaches us a new way of reading narrative, and thus creates a new kind of narrative. Benjy's section is not, strictly speaking, a stream of consciousness because Benjy's mind does not move like a stream, at least not a smooth running one. It moves in jerks, stalls at certain sights and sounds, resumes speed in response to others. By learning what provokes various responses in Benjy, we find out what constitutes his world as well as who and what he is. But in the process of composing a coherent picture, we are not just assembling information, we are acquiring and practicing the skills required to respond fruitfully to Faulkner's inversion of plot development, to what I will call the counterintuitive form of narrative pull he invents in this novel.

Sartre was the first to point out that the *The Sound and the Fury* has no future. "Everything," he says, "has already happened" (*S&F*, 267). Sartre was interested in the determinist implications of Faulkner's technique, but I am more concerned with the effect of the technique itself. As readers, we are pulled forward through this novel not by the conventional desire to find out what happens next, but by the perversely powerful need to understand why this is happening now. The novel's present consists, in other words, of events conceived not as acts with as-yet-undetermined future consequences, but as consequences already determined by as-yet-unrevealed previous events. This is what I mean by the narrative pull created by inverting the reader's normal relationship to plot. The Benjy section initiates us as readers of what seems a perverse narrative because it refuses to reward our conventional expectations as readers. We must learn to read differently, looking for answers to a different order of questions. We ask not what will this event lead to, but what is this event, what events in the past led to it and why? As we are led forward in search of answers to these questions, we find ourselves sucked into a fictional world before we can get our bearings in it. It is a kind of seduction Faulkner works, evoking both resistance and capitulation.

The Benjy section initiates this process, and in some ways epitomizes it, for Benjy is a figure of compelling sensitivity and pathos who irresistibly draws us into his experience even as he reveals its unbearability. As we read further in his section, it becomes clear that no matter how large his shadow, Benjy is eternally a little boy, and one whose only connection in or to the world is with and through his older sister Caddy, who is missing. Drawn on in our need to understand what is happening to Benjy and why, we are also drawn to him by an empathy generated by his exquisitely attuned senses and secured by our inability to stand outside his perspective. In an early scene, Benjy clings to a cold gate, awaiting Caddy's homecoming from school on the day before Christmas:

"Hello, Benjy." Caddy said. She opened the gate and came in and stooped down. Caddy smelled like leaves. "Did you come to meet me," she said. "Did you come to meet Caddy. What did you let him get his hands so cold for, Versh." "I told him to keep them in his pockets," Versh said. "Holding onto that ahun gate."

"Did you come to meet Caddy," she said, rubbing my hands. "What is it. What are you trying to tell Caddy." Caddy smelled like trees and like when she says we were asleep. (*S&F*, 4–5)

Except when he can reinhabit such memories of Caddy, and sometimes because he cannot escape from them, Benjy is in pain, continual and fundamentally irremediable pain. That pain is the more acute since Benjy cannot speak, he can only howl. For much of his section, we know he is howling, but not because that howl is itself represented on the page. Rather, we know it because others are telling him to hush, trying to make him hush, and the pressure of his felt pain is thereby heightened, sometimes to excruciating levels.

When, for example, Caddy comes home smelling of perfume rather than the usual "trees," Benjy's wail is so loud and awful that the reader wants to hurry Caddy up as she goes to the bathroom to wash it off. As Faulkner was later to say of him, "He no longer had Caddy; being an idiot he was not even aware that Caddy was missing. He knew only that something was wrong, which left a vacuum in which he grieved. He tried to fill that vacuum" (*S&F*, 233).

While we are thus drawn into Benjy's world, of course, we are picking up pieces of the puzzle that the novel as a whole will invite us to assemble. We learn that his world is populated not only by his siblings and his parents, but also by a black family headed by Dilsey and her husband Roskus. But even as we learn to identify some characters, others are blurred. For example, Quentin is Benjy's older brother, and yet another Quentin appears at certain points, one who is female. Later we will realize that this is Caddy's daughter, named after her suicidal uncle. But there is no way to know this the first time we read section one. We have to read on, assuming that mysteries will be resolved in later sections. So there is an element of suspense at work here, as there must be in any narrative. But here the suspense is resolved not by the plot's resolution, but by the reader's ability to see the gaps and fill them in when it becomes possible. On a second reading, we know there are two Quentins from the outset, and so we are in effect reading a slightly different book. This time around, we know, roughly at least, what is happening and what has happened in the past. But we are still engaged in composing and recomposing a picture, and the picture never remains the same, from section to section or from reading to reading.

Consider the next, Quentin Compson section. Here Quentin relates the events of his life on its last day, as he prepares to commit suicide by drowning himself in the Charles River in Cambridge, Massachusetts. The date is June 10, 1910, a long jump back in time from April 7, 1928, the present of section one. As his mind unravels before us, memories intrude that enable us to get a better purchase on some events only fleetingly reported in section one. Caddy's wedding, for example, came to us amid the confusion of a Benjy made drunk by Dilsey's son T.P. in the first section. Now Quentin's memory of the wedding situates Benjy's drunken memory within a more inclusive framework, but at the same time reconfigures the event in accord with Quentin's trauma instead of Benjy's.

Then she was across the porch I couldn't hear her heels then in the moonlight like a cloud, the floating shadow of the veil running across the grass, into the bellowing. She ran out of her dress, clutching her bridal, running into the bellowing where T.P. in the dew Whooey Sasprilluh Benjy under the box bellowing. (S&F, 52)

We now can better position and comprehend Benjy's experience of the wedding, but we're faced with figuring out the far more complex reaction of Quentin to it. So, as with the Benjy section, we are reading in at least two registers. One is that of the puzzle, trying to fix in our mind what is happening in the present in relation to what has happened in the past. In this register, the reader is a kind of detective in search of clues that will enable him to flush out and then flesh in the central events of the story. The other is that of the competition, say, the poker game, the ongoing effort to sustain one's defenses against the force of a voice that is sucking us into a world we can neither resist nor understand. The more we read, the more we are invested, and thus the more urgent is our need to keep reading, but also, the more dangerous our risk of losing all control or understanding.

Faulkner once described his method as a novelist by saying,

There's always a moment in experience—a thought—an incident—that's there. Then all I do is work up to that moment. I figure what must have happened before to lead people to that particular moment, and I work away from it, finding out how people act after the moment. (S&F, 373)

For Quentin Compson, such an "incident" is the discovery that his sister has lost her virginity while he remains himself a virgin. From this follows his frantic and failed effort to avenge her honor by shooting her lover Dalton Ames and his equally frantic and failed effort to have sex with her himself. He ultimately imagines himself telling his father that he and Caddy have committed incest, so as to make it, somehow, retroactively true. Faulkner "works up to" this moment, exploring the failure of the Compson parents to provide the love and care they should, and thereby leaving Dilsey and Caddy with the responsibilities of both fathering and mothering. But simultaneously, he works away from it, tracking Quentin's unrelentingly self-destructive course, as well as the breakdown of the Compson family at large.

That breakdown is further inflected in the final two sections of the novel. Jason Compson, the speaker in the third section, provides a kind of dark comic relief to the intensities of the first two. "Once a bitch always a bitch, what I say," he begins (*S&F*, 113). Like his brothers, he is both symptom and victim of a deeply fractured family, but unlike them, he squarely blames his sister for his own failures. Her husband, Herbert Head, an Indiana banker, was to have given Jason a job in his bank. When Herbert divorces Caddy on discovering that she is pregnant, he also withdraws the job offer. Accordingly, Jason can spend the rest of his life acting out his revenge on his sister, largely by mistreating her daughter Quentin, but also by stealing the money Caddy sends to support her. Relocating us in the present of April 6, 1928, the Jason section clarifies a good deal, largely because Jason is so plainspoken and unreflective. But the price we pay for clarification is a high one: we have to spend a good deal of time listening to Jason, who is certainly among the most repugnant figures in all literature. We may for a while enjoy the relief of hearing some one speak colloquially, but sooner or later we realize that he seems to be talking to himself all the time. Although Faulkner was ironically to call him the "first sane Compson since before Culloden," Jason emerges as a virtual madman, so charged with anger and resentment is he (*S&F*, 212). If grief and empathy bonded us with Benjy, and despair and confusion descend on us with Quentin, a kind of moral nausea sets in with Jason, and nowhere more keenly than when he is funny. Here is Jason confronting Luster and Benjy in the same setting in which we've seen them in section one:

> "Take him on round to the back," I says. "What the hell makes you want to keep him around here where people can see him?" I made them go on, before he got started bellowing good. It's bad enough on Sundays, with that dam field full of people that haven't got a side show and six niggers to feed, knocking a dam oversize mothball around. He's going to keep on running up and down that fence and bellowing every time they come in sight until the first thing I know they're going to begin charging me golf dues, then Mother and Dilsey'll have to get a couple of china door knobs and a walking stick and work it out, unless I play at night with a lantern. (*S&F*, 117–118)

Jason distances himself from the scene he confronts by cozying up to us and making fun of it, but the more he does so, the more we want to shove him away. It is a distinct pleasure when Jason is foiled by Caddy's daughter Quentin in the novel's final section, but meanwhile it is a sharp relief just getting beyond the sound of his voice.

Reinforcing that relief is the calm serenity with which a third person narrator begins section four: "The day dawned bleak and chill" (*S&F*, 165). Often referred to as the "Dilsey" section, because Dilsey plays such a central role in its action, the final part of the novel is actually narrated by an authoritative, not to mention eloquent, voice. Entitled April 8, 1928, the fourth section of the novel is set on the Easter Sunday following the April 6th of Jason's section and the April 7th of Benjy's. The story unfolds in a simple, straightforward time sequence, beginning with Dilsey's early morning emergence and continuing through the family's discovery that Quentin has run away with one of the circus men and stolen Jason's hoarded money, through the black church service to which Dilsey takes Benjy. That service itself serves as the epiphany of the section as well as the novel, taking us into the community of black residents as they listen to an Easter sermon. The Christian symbolism of the Passion Week is foregrounded in the church service, and Dilsey's visionary insight is expressed in and because of her faith. When she says she has seen the first and the last, the beginning and the ending, she speaks with the authority of Revelation in her understanding of both the Compson family history and God's plan of salvation, even though the two do not match up.

In one sense, we are provided with what Frank Kermode has called a "sense of an ending," the crucial closure to a narrative that retrospectively provides order and coherence.[19] For Kermode, as for Faulkner here, the Christian story is the mythic model for all Western narrative. Christ is born into the human world in medias res and thereby is the tragic protagonist of a world-changing story. This story redeems all history, providing human life with meaning and value; in dividing BC from AD, it punctuates time, ordering it into myth. Dilsey's grasp of such an order is both authentic and fully articulated in the final section of the novel. But at the same time, this order is recast as at best inaccessible and at worst irrelevant to the human lives it ostensibly shelters and redeems. Modernist irony returns with a vengeance as Faulkner describes the church. As Dilsey and Benjy approach it, the "weathered church lifted its crazy steeple like a painted church, and the whole scene was as flat and without perspective as a painted cardboard set upon the ultimate edge of the flat earth, against the windy sunlight of space and April and a midmorning filled with bells" (*S&F*, 182). Whatever order and meaning has been found, it is both fragile and artificially produced. The novel's ending only reiterates this ironic viewpoint when it portrays Benjy as howling in protest because the carriage he's riding in has turned in the wrong direction around the town square. Once the carriage is turned in the right direction, Benjy hushes, "his eyes . . . empty and blue and serene again as cornice and façade flowed smoothly once more from left to right, post and tree, window and doorway and signboard each in its ordered place" (*S&F*, 199). The value of order itself is under suspicion if all it amounts to is an arbitrary sequence. Indeed, the title of the novel already suggests the possibility that any story, any narrative that weaves a meaningful pattern is in the end arbitrary, a "tale told by an idiot, full of sound and fury signifying nothing" (*Macbeth*, 5, 5, 25–27).

In one of his many accounts of writing *The Sound and the Fury*, Faulkner used an unusual locution as he reiterated his familiar litany: "So I wrote Quentin's and Jason's sections, trying to clarify Benjy's. But I saw that I was merely temporizing; That I should have to get completely out of the book." Actually, Faulkner didn't really want "to get completely out of the book"

(*S&F*, 231). He "realized that there would be compensations, that in a sense [he] could then give a final turn to the screw and extract some ultimate distillation." Nevertheless, "it took [him] better than a month to take pen and write *The day dawned bleak and chill*" because finishing the book would mean losing touch with "perhaps the only thing in literature that would move [him] very much: Caddy climbing the pear tree" (*S&F*, 227). In fact, there is a sense in which Faulkner never fully "got out of" *The Sound and the Fury*. For one thing, until the end of his life, he clearly never tired of repeating the story of its composition. More revealing for our purposes is the fact that he was ready and eager almost sixteen years later to add another section, called "Appendix/Compson, 1699–1945," for Malcolm Cowley's *The Viking Portable Faulkner* in 1946.

As the dating in its title indicates, the Appendix is actually a combination sequel and prequel, organized as a roughly chronological series of names, by no means all of them Compson. Before getting to the characters with whom we are familiar, for example, the Appendix treats one Ikkemotubbe, "a dispossessed American king" who sold his land and led his Chickasaw tribe west to Oklahoma, as well as Andrew Jackson, "a great white father with a sword" (*S&F*, 203–204). Prompted at least in part by Cowley's aim in his anthology to foreground Yoknapatawpha County as the unifying framework for his career, Faulkner resituated the Compson story against the backdrop of the larger social history he had begun to imagine in *Sartoris,* and subsequently written into life in *Light in August, Absalom, Absalom!,* and *Go Down, Moses,* among other novels and stories he had published between 1929 and 1946. He was thoroughly excited at the results of his labor. Called upon for a short synopsis, he sent Cowley the longer manuscript, saying, "I should have done this when I wrote the book. Then the whole thing would have fallen into pattern like a jigsaw puzzle when the magician's wand touched it."[20] A few years later he made the same point about the Appendix in recommending its publication at the beginning of a new edition of *The Sound and the Fury*, telling his editor at Random House that "it is the key to the whole book, and after reading it, the 4 sections as they stand now fall into clarity and place" (*SL*, 203). Actually, as generations of readers have discovered, the Appendix is by no means such a "key." A fascinating piece of writing, and a provocative gloss on the novel proper, it actually distorts it by superimposing on it a vast genealogical past that the novel as written in no way requires.

Which is not to say that Faulkner meant to mislead Cowley. For Faulkner, composing the Appendix clearly did make the novel's pieces fall into their proper place in the "puzzle." It's just that the puzzle in question is no longer primarily the one proffered by *The Sound and the Fury,* but more importantly, the puzzle of his whole career, the Balzacian invention of a world. Cowley has been criticized on occasion for overemphasizing the importance of Yoknapatawpha, Faulkner's much celebrated "cosmos of [his] own," thereby initiating a tendency to under-estimate the value of works not set there.[21] But Cowley deserves a good deal of credit, and not only for republishing Faulkner's work when it was largely out of print. By inviting Faulkner to see himself as "Sole Owner and Proprieter" of a whole imagined world rather than simply a typewriter, Cowley afforded him a renewed and much needed venue for recognizing himself as an author (*S&F*, 216–217). So much is clear from a passage later in the same letter, where Faulkner says of the Appendix, "I think this is all right, it took me about a week to get Hollywood out of my lungs, but I am still writing all right, I believe" (*FCF*, 37). Since he had been in and out of Hollywood for the past ten years and had not published a novel since 1942, it was no small relief that he was "still writing." He closed by asking Cowley to tell him what he thinks of the Appendix. "I think it is really pretty good," Faulkner admits, "to stand as it is, as a piece without implications" (*FCF*, 37).

Faulkner's enthusiasm here, I am suggesting, is partly the effect of re-seeing his work as all of a piece, as an ongoing Balzacian act of invention. Cowley's insistent focus on this unifying perspective enabled Faulkner to remember and review his invented world as a whole thing, one perhaps even still under construction. But his excitement is more immediately grounded in his success at reentering his favorite novel, the one he had tried to "get completely out of." This experience generated a "piece without implications," one that could "stand as it is" because it proved he could still write with passion. In this respect it is, I think, no accident that the longest and most dramatically developed section in the Appendix concerns Caddy.

In writing the Appendix, Faulkner was making another at-tempt at what he claimed always to be doing, "trying to put it all between one Cap and one period," even though he admitted, "I don't know how to do it. All I know to do is to keep on trying in a new way" (*FCF*, 14). But lest the Appendix confuse us, it is well to recall that he was already practicing this art form in *The Sound and the Fury*. Here, he tried four times to put it all between one Cap and one period, and as he liked to say, "failed" each time. But in the process he broke new ground both for himself as writer and for the novel as form. In the next decade, he would not only populate his invented world with a host of characters from all social ranks, but he would enlarge the creative possibilities of the novel as decisively as had Conrad and Joyce before him.

Two

THE MAJOR PHASE, PART 1: *AS I LAY DYING, SANCTUARY,* AND *LIGHT IN AUGUST*

ON JUNE 20, 1929, FAULKNER MARRIED ESTELLE OLDHAM. He would soon turn thirty-two and Estelle was thirty-three years old. Recently divorced, Estelle brought two children, aged five and ten, to the marriage, along with her own anxieties and misgivings. Judging from what his biographers have reported, Faulkner was deeply ambivalent about this decision, and Estelle was sufficiently distraught while on her honeymoon that summer that she attempted suicide. The marriage was always to be a difficult one, intermittently a disaster, not least because both were alcoholics. But Faulkner's bond with Estelle was clearly a profound one, and his love for her children strengthened that bond, as did the birth of their daughter, Jill, on June 24, 1933. (Their first child, Alabama, was born prematurely on January 11, 1931, and died at the age of nine days, an event whose traumatic impact on both was severe.) Much has been written about Faulkner's troubled marriage, especially about how it could have lasted the rest of his life, given the torment it brought to both husband and wife. In my view, we are not likely ever to answer this question. In Faulkner's view, it would be none of our business anyway. What we can say, I think, is that in part what sustained the marriage was Faulkner's social identification as a father, and not only as Jill's.

Faulkner's own father died before Jill was born, and from that day, August 7, 1932, Faulkner assumed responsibility for a good many members of his continually extending family. In addition to his mother and her two black servants, Estelle and her two children, he was eventually to support his brother Dean's wife when Dean was killed in a plane crash in 1935, as well as the daughter born of that marriage two months after Dean's death. As the oldest son, Faulkner apparently never doubted that he was destined to inherit the role of patriarch. Although Cornell Franklin provided some economic support for Estelle's children, Faulkner had now to make a real living. He was eventually to bear a large economic burden as head of the Falkner family. In carrying that burden, however, Faulkner was fulfilling what he understood to be a distinctively masculine responsibility. In marrying Estelle, buying an old plantation house he renamed Rowan Oak, and becoming Jill's father, he was again building on the model of his great-grandfather, not only as writer now, but as a patriarch in his own right.

That model, of course, by no means precluded "philandering," a male family tradition which, like drinking, Faulkner did his part to keep up. Within a few years of Jill's birth, he began an affair with Meta Carpenter, whom he met while working for Howard Hawks in Hollywood in 1935. Although she married someone else, their relationship persisted in various forms for fifteen years. Faulkner could not bring himself finally to leave his wife for Meta, saying that Estelle would take Jill away from him if he did. He might or might not have been fully truthful in this claim, but he was certainly choosing not to marry again and not to abandon his position as father. Remaining married to Estelle ironically secured a certain familiar kind of male freedom. Faulkner liked to see himself as a man who pursued women, and he liked it even more when they began to respond positively, as they did far more often as he became more successful and secure, not to mention handsome. He was still pursuing them after Jill had grown up and left home in the 1950s. But he was also still the family patriarch.

It is against this biographical backdrop, then, that I want to focus on the years in which Faulkner produced his greatest work, 1929–1942. Now resolved to be a novelist, Faulkner was faced with a new conflict. On the one hand, he was a father with a growing financial responsibility to a large family. On the other, he was a writer with a growing reputation among critics as an important modern novelist. His problem, in other words, was how to continue in the path opened to him by the writing of *The Sound and the Fury* and at the same time maintain his increasingly weighty role as head of the family. Over the next fifteen years, he would try to solve this problem both by selling short stories and by spending a good part of his time in Hollywood, where at least during the 1930s he could command a good salary. But throughout this period, the conflicting demands of writing the novels he sought to write and fulfilling his obligations to his family required of him an almost superhuman exercise of will and determination.

The Sound and the Fury was published on October 7, 1929, and received mixed notices. Some reviewers chimed in with a general complaint about the difficulties of modern fiction in general, grouping Faulkner with Joyce and Woolf as unnecessarily obfuscatory. But to be criticized as one of this company was of course automatically to be elevated to the domain of serious literature. Others, such as Henry Nash Smith, recognized originality in the novel and saw it as the harbinger of a great career in the making. "No matter how universal the standard, there are certain pages in this novel which are very near great literature," Smith said, and went on to compare Faulkner's genius to that of Chaucer.[1] Gratifying though this recognition was, it did not change the fact that the novel did not sell well. But neither his new publisher, Hal Smith, nor Faulkner had expected good sales. After all, *Sartoris,* published ten months earlier in January 1929, had met with limited success both critically and financially. So Faulkner was prepared with another ploy. In the spring months of 1929, as *The Sound and the Fury* was being copyedited, he wrote a new novel in the hope of making money. It was called *Sanctuary.*

As with *The Sound and the Fury,* Faulkner would comment repeatedly on this novel, although with a distinctly different slant. "I made a thorough and methodical study of everything on the list of best-sellers. When I thought I knew what the public wanted, I decided to give them a little more than they had been getting; stronger and rawer—more brutal. Guts and genitals" (Blotner, 233–234). The key event of the novel is the rape of a young co-ed, Temple Drake, by an impotent though lethal gangster named Popeye, who uses a corncob in place of a phallus, and then takes Temple to a Memphis brothel where he matches her up with a gambler named Red so as to play the voyeur, moaning as he watches the two of them copulate from the end of her bed. When she read it, Estelle complained, "It's horrible." "It's meant to be," Faulkner replied. "It will sell." His publisher, however, at first disagreed. According to Faulkner, Hal Smith said, "Good God, I can't publish this. We'd both be in jail" (Blotner, 239). The novel remained on hold until after Faulkner had written and published *As I Lay Dying* in 1930, but was indeed published in 1931, albeit with substantial revisions which Faulkner insisted on and paid for, saying that he could not allow the novel to appear in its original form.

Sanctuary has received especially keen critical scrutiny as a result of its birth in sin and its rebirth in glory. Noel Polk, who restored and published the earlier, unrevised version of the novel in 1981 has persuasively demonstrated that whatever Faulkner's motives, the original manuscript displays his usual careful craftsmanship and thus should not be regarded as a slipshod potboiler. Along with other distinguished Faulkner critics, especially Michael Millgate and Joseph Blotner, Polk treats Faulkner's sardonic account of the novel's sordid financial motives as "misleading."[2] In his introduction to a 1932 Random House reprinting of the novel Faulkner began by calling the novel "a cheap idea, because it was deliberately conceived to make money," but still concluded by saying, "I hope you will buy it and tell your friends and I hope they will buy it too."[3] Certainly Polk is right to see Faulkner distancing himself from the novel and its audience so as to underscore his aesthetic integrity. He explains that he has revised the novel so as "to make out of it something which would not shame *The Sound and the Fury* and *As I Lay Dying*" (*Sanctuary*, 324). What Polk also helps us to recognize, however, is that just because Faulkner had set out to make money with the novel doesn't mean he would have been careless in writing it. Nor was his financial motive necessarily suspended by his scrupulous revisions. As it turned out, his prediction was right; the novel did indeed sell. And as he knew all too well, it sold primarily because it was sensationally horrifying. (In Oxford, people bought the novel at the local drugstore, although they insisted on having it wrapped in brown paper so as to hide their deed.) As both Polk and Millgate have made clear, Faulkner's revisions tightened and improved the novel, but they did not downplay its graphic treatment of sex, murder, and brutality. On the contrary, the final version of the novel foregrounds and intensifies these elements.[4]

Sanctuary, as André Malraux was to say in later years, represents "the intrusion of Greek tragedy into the detective story" (Blotner, 276). Faulkner was quite familiar with the gangster and detective fiction of his era, and he used that knowledge to rich effect in *Sanctuary.* Like Dashiell Hammett, whose work he admired, Faulkner portrayed a sordid and violent underworld, but instead of sending in a Continental Op or a Sam Spade to combat the forces of evil, Faulkner sent Horace Benbow, the glassblowing, impotent, and incestuous aesthete he had imported from *Flags in the Dust.* Horace is both detective and lawyer, but his idealized devotion to justice renders him incapable of facing up to what Hammett's detectives always have to recognize eventually—not only the deep and constitutive corruption of the world but also their complicity in it. Set in the present, *Sanctuary*'s events take place in Jefferson, Memphis, and Frenchman's Bend, all to become familiar sites in Faulkner's fiction. But the novel is distinctive in its nihilistic vision, obsessively focused on the dark and sinister world lurking just beneath the hypocritical bourgeois surfaces of society, whether urban or rural.

Critics were quick to see its debt to the hard-boiled school of fiction as well as to the anti-idealist or "naturalist" tradition from Theodore Dreiser to Erskine Caldwell. Recognizing Faulkner's talent, they recoiled at the "ghastly details of human depravity" on which he dwelled (Inge, 59). In an influential review, Henry Seidel Canby aligned Faulkner with "the sadistic school" of literature, calling him "cruel with a cool and interested cruelty," and harboring a "hatred that is neither passionate nor the result of thwarting, but calm, reasoned, and complete" (Inge, 56). Although misleading as an account of Faulkner's later fiction, Canby's response highlights what is distinctive about *Sanctuary*, its success at using language with exquisite sensitivity and grace to create scenes and characters of irremediable ugliness and misery. One can't dismiss it as pulp fiction; it is too brilliantly written. A fierce and cold portrayal of human depravity and injustice, the novel is as chiseled in its formal execution as it is devastating in its social critique. But one can't comfortably situate it within the constellation of Faulkner's greatest fiction because it is indeed sadistic, and primarily toward its readers, whom Faulkner seems to have regarded—as his 1932 Introduction suggests—with anger and contempt. It is not only a question of exposing the hypocrisy of the townspeople, who are all too ready to lie and lynch in order not to face the truth. It is almost as if Faulkner regarded his readers as sharing the townspeople's attitudes and were out to rub our faces in the dirt. In a sense, we are positioned to be shocked, as is Temple Drake, confronted with a relentless barrage of threat and disgust.

For example, finding herself alone at Frenchman's Bend, thrust suddenly into a world of bootleggers, gangsters, and idiots, Temple is terrified and confides in Ruby, an ex-prostitute and common-law wife of Lee Goodwin, the boss of the moonshine business. "I'm not afraid," Temple said. "Things like that don't happen. Do they? They're just like other people. You're just like other people. With a little baby." Ruby replies with contempt, "Like what people?" (*Sanctuary,* 56). A hard-bitten and brutalized woman, Ruby looks on with condescension and contempt as Temple runs frantically in and out of the house, provoking the very sexual danger she fears. As mother and child, Ruby and her baby resemble a grotesque pietà, a kind of wretched expressionist parody of the sentimental picture Temple tries to project. Ruby's baby is kept in a cardboard box beside the stove. When periodically it awakens, "its lead-colored eyelids show . . . a thin line of eyeball" (*Sanctuary,* 56). Any illusions we may harbor about the sacred bonds of family are shattered, and it is the almost physical sensation of the shattering that the novel strives to effect in its reader.

Even those reviews that expressed shock at *Sanctuary* praised its author for his narrative mastery. Calling the story "too much of an evil thing," for example, one reviewer nevertheless described Faulkner himself as "the most gifted novelist writing in the United States" (Inge, 53). Thanks to the novel's success, a collection of short stories, *These Thirteen,* was published in the fall of 1931, and Faulkner was soon lionized in New York City and Charlottesville, Viriginia, where he met and mingled with the literary celebrities of the day. Although, thanks to the demands of restoring his new house, Rowan Oak, he was still in debt, Faulkner was at last in demand.

It is important to note, however, that the critical esteem Faulkner now commanded was due at least as much to *As I Lay Dying* as to *Sanctuary*. Certainly *As I Lay Dying*, published ahead of *Sanctuary* in 1930, is a more ambitious work and indisputably one of his finest, as Faulkner himself knew. He said of it, "Before I began I said, I am going to write a book by which, at a pinch, I can stand or fall if I never touch ink again" (Minter, 117). He was fond of describing the novel as a *"tour de force. I took this family and subjected them to the two greatest catastrophes which man can suffer—flood and fire, that's all"*[5] (87). He also liked to point out that unlike *The Sound and the Fury, As I Lay Dying* was entirely premeditated. This time he had a plan. "I knew," he said, "when I put down the first word what the last word of that would be. . . . I wrote [it] in about six weeks without changing any of it" (*University*, 207). As usual, Faulkner's tale here is not entirely accurate. He did not write the novel in six weeks, but he did write it with amazing dispatch, beginning on October 29, 1929, and completing the revised typescript by January 12, 1930 (Minter, 120). And although he did make revisions, he made remarkably few, given how radical the novel's narrative procedures are. Some readers believe it his greatest novel. Certainly it represents another astonishing leap forward in Faulkner's ongoing experiments with form.

Like *The Sound and the Fury, As I Lay Dying* focuses on a family, but the Bundrens differ appreciably from the Compsons. Anse and his wife Addie Bundren are tenant farmers living forty miles from Jefferson in the rural backwaters of what is for the first time identified by name as Yoknapatawpha County. They have four sons and a daughter, children whose names signal the country origins distinguishing them from the Compsons: Cash,

Darl, Jewel, Dewey Dell, and Vardaman. The central event in the novel is Addie Bundren's death, which initiates the family's journey to Jefferson where she has asked to be buried. In the course of this trip, we learn the history of the Bundrens' marriage, including Addie's adulterous affair with the Reverend Whitfield, of which Jewel is the fruit. We learn that Dewey Dell has become pregnant shortly before her mother's death. But the conflicts and anxieties that both split and bond the Bundrens stem from no socially consequent past. In other words, there is no extended family history to be addressed, as in the Appendix to *The Sound and the Fury*. Rather, as the Bundrens make their way by mule-driven wagon toward Jefferson, they gradually encounter cars and other signs of townspeople, stretching the novel's focus to incorporate town and country and to document the differences between them. Although similarly insular in its primary concern with a nuclear family, *As I Lay Dying* stretches its reach to map a larger geographical social terrain than does *The Sound and the Fury*.

Further, there is a fundamental difference between the ways in which the two novels tell their stories. *The Sound and the Fury* is, in one sense, a technically simpler book to read than *As I Lay Dying*. In its original form, without the Appendix, *The Sound and the Fury* asks the reader to inhabit four successive points of view in order to compose the story of the Compson family. The final section is crucial to this enterprise, as it provides a detached, omniscient perspective from which we can assemble the pieces of the story retrospectively. That stance—outside the book, so to speak—allows us to integrate what we have seen from a single, detached viewpoint. *As I Lay Dying* is conceptually more complex. It consists not in four sections, each with its own distinctive point of view, but rather in fifty-nine monologues spoken by fifteen different characters. Instead of a gradually emerging group of characters set against a gradually emerging background, we have a field of interacting figures recurrently emerging out of a flux. Never allowed to settle for long into any character's consciousness, frustrated in our endeavor to form an image of more than passing instants, we are less confronted with the world of the novel than pulled through it along with the Bundrens. Because there is no detached much less omniscient narrator, we are at the mercy of the individual viewpoints in our effort to get some purchase on what is happening. This makes for a radically different reading experience. Faulkner is now using multiple perspective to present events not just as seen by different characters but as themselves constituted by subjects and objects interacting in a flux presided over by no third person perspective at all.

To make matters even more formidable, the controlling time frame of the novel is a continuous present. Already in motion as we join it, the story told here begins the day before Addie Bundren dies and closes ten days later with the Bundrens' departure from Jefferson, having finally buried a rotting corpse in the cemetery there. Within this time period, however, events by no means unfold in precise chronological order. There are many flashbacks within the monologues, and Addie's death itself is not a punctual event but one experienced continually by various characters before it is fully accomplished—indeed, in order for it to be fully accomplished. As Dr. Peabody puts it, "When I was young, I believed death to be a phenomenon of the body; now I know it to be merely a function of the mind— and that of the minds of the ones who suffer bereavement."[6]

As represented in this novel, however, death concerns both the body and the mind, and in particular the contradictions attendant upon human beings having both. As Eric Sundquist has shown, the problem presented by the mother's death is that for her sons especially she is both there and not there; her body remains, her self is missing.[7] That contradiction is reflected formally in the fact that Addie herself speaks after her death has apparently occurred. Thus, the novel's title, *As I Lay Dying,* offers a critical clue to its peculiar form. Addie's death is less an event than it is a process, a "phenomenon" the experience of which requires everyone in the family to find some resolution.

The title quotes from Book XI of the *Odyssey,* where Agamemnon tells Odysseus the story of his own death at the hands of his wife Clytemnestra. As Faulkner recited the speech, Agamemnon says, "As I lay dying the woman with the dog's eyes would not close my eyes for me as I descended into Hades" (Blotner, 248–249). Like Agamemnon, Addie Bundren speaks from a kind of netherworld, beyond death but not yet wholly beyond reach. The Homeric allusion does not suggest the kind of allegorical parallels that Joyce exploited in *Ulysses* but instead invites us to focus on the act of dying as it is happening, and as a social, a psychological, and a physical process. It also underscores the importance of funeral rituals as a means of suturing the wound in life that death inflicts on both the dead and the living. Clytemnestra stands condemned not only for killing her husband but for refusing to close his eyes in peace, to afford him the respect he deserves. Addie Bundren, on the contrary, is treated to an elaborate funeral procession, but one which is by no means emblematic of respect. As she lies dying, she watches her eldest son Cash through the window as he builds her coffin.

Once dead, her body is laid in that coffin with her head at its foot, so that her wedding gown can spread out at the coffin's head. Her youngest son bores two holes through the coffin into her head, in order for her to breathe. Her coffin is almost lost as the wagon it rides in is overturned and the mules that pull it are drowned crossing a flooded river. Buzzards increase in number and proximity as her body gives off a growing stench in the course of a six-day journey. She is almost burned in a barn, when her second son Darl sets it on fire. And within hours of her final burial in Jefferson, she has been replaced by a new "Mrs. Bundren."

The extended and grotesque funeral procession, then, is a travesty of bereavement, carried out by Anse Bundren on the grounds that he promised Addie he would take her to Jefferson to be buried, but driven by his desire to secure a new set of teeth and a new wife. Dewey Dell is equally committed to this mockery of faithful memorialization because she is pregnant and seeks an abortion, which she hopes somehow to get in town. Vardaman, too young to understand what has happened, and thus the locus of some of the novel's most bizarre and moving moments, is promised a sight of the electric train he once saw in a storefront window at Christmas. As it turns out, he has to make do with bananas, the other desirable object unavailable except in town. But while the social convention of the funeral is rendered a farce, the journey through which that convention is fulfilled becomes an epic of mourning. Whatever their individual aims or interests, each member of the Bundren family must perform the work of mourning. In Freud's phrasing, they must disconnect from the lost object and regain a sense of individual wholeness. The family as well must change and adapt in order to compensate for its lost center; its members must struggle with each other and the natural world around them in order to reestablish both their individual identities and their family relations. The novel both represents and enacts this process, embodying a powerful and moving drama in the course of which fundamental questions are brought into play, questions about life and death, mind and body, word and deed, mine and yours.

The structuring of the novel as a set of monologues signals the alienation of each character, underscoring the thematic issue of connection and disconnection. Although dialogues are represented within some of the monologues, the novel itself exists exclusively in monologue form, a form that is private by nature. When Vardaman says, "My mother is a fish," he is not speaking to anyone except himself. The sense of isolation within which people can and often do live their lives is heightened by the separate monologues in which the characters are represented. This strategy has important consequences for us as well. The reader experiences each character in two ways: first, from within, as he or she thinks aloud, and second, during other monologues, from outside, as he or she is seen, commented upon, or addressed by, another character. But we never experience any character as we would from the vantage point of a third person omniscient narrative—that is, from both within and without at the same time. One might argue that even in conventional narratives this is the case, since even an omniscient narrator can't be in two places at once, thus normally taking us inside a character's thoughts and experiences for a while, and then shifting to an external perspective or to another character's mind. But in such conventional narratives, we at least have the illusion of being both within and without in the course of the novel. In *As I Lay Dying*, this illusion is denied us. In *Middlemarch*, for example, we are invited to roam freely between characters' thoughts and the world they inhabit, while in Faulkner's novel, we are reminded with each new monologue of the gap between character and character, as well as between character and world. The "between" is foregrounded as a problem, a gap that must be filled in. The world, both natural and social, in a sense springs into being with each monologue, and vanishes beneath it as it ends. It is up to us to relate character to character and characters to the world they share, much as it is up to each character to connect himself or herself to other selves, and to both natural and social worlds.

Darl, Addie's mad and clairvoyant son, provides the most dramatic example of this struggle. Darl lies awake "in a strange room," trying to assure himself that he will still exist even after he goes to sleep. It takes him a long paragraph of careful and circular reasoning to arrive at the conclusion that he does exist: "I must be, or I could not empty myself for sleep in a strange room. And so, if I am not emptied yet, I am *is*" (*AILD*, 80–81). Crucial to Darl's final, though of course temporary, success here is the sound of the rain, which he imagines "shaping the wagon that is ours, the load that is no longer theirs that felled and sawed it nor yet theirs that bought it and which is not ours either, lie on our wagon though it does." For all the elaborate convolutions of is and was, are and are not, once Darl proves to himself that the wagon is real, he is able to argue his way to the needed conclusion that he is real as well. For Darl, unlike Shakespeare's Hamlet, the question is not whether to be or not to be; it is whether you are in the first place.

Like Quentin Compson, Darl Bundren invites us to speculate on Faulkner's own anxieties as an adolescent. Certainly he experienced severe moments of existential self-doubt well into his twenties, as his poetry amply demonstrates. But we need to be careful in our assessment of such similarities. Faulkner by now had achieved a critical distance on such psychic threats. Similarly, we could "explain" Darl's situation by drawing on theoretical models such as psychoanalysis. Emotionally rejected by his mother, we could say, he has been psychologically unhinged all his life; his mother's death only calls up and exacerbates this condition.

But any such psychoanalytical "explanation" of Darl's condition remains largely marginal to what makes him such a powerful figure in this novel, his constant need to bring himself into the world and the world into being by connecting them. Much as Benjy's retarded mind enabled Faulkner to present the world of *The Sound and the Fury* in a particular way—as made up of images and sensations left unplotted by any maturation process—Darl's brilliant madness makes him the site of an ongoing struggle to make himself and his world cohere. Always uncertain of his own being, he is compelled to reach out and connect with the world through a vividly sensory imagination in order to know that he "is." In thus reaching out, he imagines, as here, scenes he cannot actually see. His family complains that his "eyes" are always "full of the land," and so they are, since he is forced into clairvoyance by his need to connect (*AILD*, 27). Darl's clairvoyance also, of course, proves essential to Faulkner's narrative strategy as it enables him to represent scenes from the vantage point of someone not present at them but in charge of a rich interpretive filter, thereby substituting for the missing omniscient narrator. Without Darl, the novel would have to depend too heavily on flashbacks, impeding the sense of relentless forward motion it sustains.

Without Darl, further, we would have little insight into his brothers Jewel and Cash, both of whom act a good deal more than they speak. The one monologue Jewel delivers makes clear that he is in a rage at his family for the way in which it is treating his dying mother, especially Cash, "hammering and sawing on that goddamn box. Where she's got to see him." Jewel certainly has a point; there is something perverse about Cash's performance for his mother, as if he were saying "See what a good one I am making for you" (*AILD*, 14). But Cash is actually trying to show respect for his mother, just as Jewel and Darl do, each in his own strange fashion.

An obsessively careful and much admired carpenter in his local region, Cash mourns his mother's death in the only way he can—by building her a perfect coffin. In one of his few monologues, Cash explains in thirteen numbered sentences why he made the coffin "on the bevel," beginning with "1. There is more surface for the nails to grip," and ending with, "13. It makes a neater job" (*AILD*, 82–83). In his own way, the sane and calm Cash is as committed to rationality as the mad Darl is, and as dependent on the material world for a sense of his and its reality. But Cash thinks and works within a precise and narrow framework, relying on a basically literal-minded reading of the world. For example, as Jewel reports, when Cash was a little boy, Addie one day said that "if she had some fertilizer she would try to raise some flowers," whereupon Cash "taken the bread pan and brought it back from the barn full of dung" (*AILD*, 14). He has broken a leg falling off a church steeple while repairing it and can tell people exactly how far he fell, "twenty-eight foot, four and a half inches, about" (*AILD*, 90). Once it is clear to him that Addie is dying, Cash is wholly focused on the box he is building for her, holding up each plank for her approval before nailing it down. His single-mindedness is at once laudable and outrageous. No wonder Jewel cries, "Good God, do you want to see her in it?" (*AILD*, 14). But what Jewel can't recognize is the loving concern Cash has invested in this beautifully constructed box. Vernon Tull, a neighbor, can't see it either, but he can admire Cash's devotion to his craft. After Vardaman has drilled two holes in the coffin top, Cash carves plugs for them, "one at a time, the wood wet and hard to work." As Vernon notes, he "could cut up a tin can and hide the holes and nobody wouldn't know the difference" (*AILD*, 87). Cash has found in craftsmanship a way of being in the world, and it provides his only means of relating to that world. Its limits are clear; Cash, for example, rationalizes sending Darl to the asylum in Jackson on the grounds that in burning down Gillespie's barn, he destroyed property. On the other hand, Cash's limits do not preclude his stoic capacity for suffering or his touching affection for the music he hears on the "graphophone." Nor do they keep him from understanding why Darl burned the barn, even if he can't finally approve of it. "Of course it was Jewel's horse was traded to get her that nigh to town," he reasons in his instrumental way, and therefore "in a sense it was the value of his horse Darl tried to burn up." But he also questions the correctness of what his reason tells him: "when Darl seen that it looked like one of us would have to do something, I can almost believe he done right in a way" (*AILD*, 233).

It is this capacity for doubt, for questioning even the grounds of one's own judgment, that Jewel lacks. Jewel apparently lives in a constant state of outrage, almost bringing on a fight with people on the road as they enter Jefferson, ready to leap on Darl as soon as the family has decided he must be evicted to Jackson. Since puberty, his horse has provided his only viable means of connecting with his world. One of the wild herd of ponies brought into Yoknapatawpha by a Texas horse trader in the story "Spotted Horses," Jewel's horse remains nameless and essentially wild, affording him a worthy opponent and comrade in the physical battle that is his life. Incapable of calm, much less contemplation, Jewel actually resembles his horse in being only barely under control most of the time. Jewel is particularly hostile to Darl because Darl taunts him with questions like "Do you know she is going to die, Jewel?" and ironic jabs like "It's not your horse that's dead, Jewel" (*AILD*, 39, 94). As Faulkner was to confirm, Jewel doesn't necessarily know that he is not Anse's son (*University*, 109). But Darl knows and thus realizes why Jewel is his mother's favorite, making his own sense of alienation the more unbearable. But Jewel's anger at Darl stems from the same source as his anger at the world, the sense of violation he feels from everything that stands outside and thereby threatens his bond first with his mother, and then with his horse. Clinging violently to his invaded but still precious privacy, Jewel turns his "wooden" back to the world, flinging out nothing but curses, "Goddamn you," "Pick up, goddamn your thick-nosed soul to hell, pick up" (*AILD*, 95, 97).

Dewey Dell is hostile to Darl, as she too feels her privacy violated by his clairvoyance. But in her case, there is something to hide—her pregnant condition. What Darl knows about Jewel may or may not be actually known to Jewel, but Dewey Dell certainly knows she is pregnant, "because God gave women a sign when something has happened bad" (*AILD*, 58). Knowing that Darl knows "without the words," Dewey Dell feels exposed and naked in his eyes, making her terror all the more acute (*AILD*, 27). But she would like to have Darl's capacity for wordless communication with Dr. Peabody. "He could fix it all right, if he just would. And he don't even know it. He could do everything for me if he just knowed it" (*AILD*, 63). To Dr. Peabody, Dewey Dell is a daughter to be comforted and a cook to provide him with food; to Dewey Dell, Dr. Peabody is a potential source of salvation, if he only knew. The split between interior and exterior, between characters' private experience and their public affect is particularly dramatic here. In so fiercely focusing on what the doctor could do for her, Dewey Dell exacerbates her own isolation. "It's because I am alone," she says. "If I could just feel it, it would be different because I would not be alone." But immediately she recognizes the paradox of her situation: "But if I were not alone, everybody would know it" (*AILD*, 58–59). If she could feel the baby inside her, she would have company, as it were. But if she could feel the baby inside her, her pregnancy would be showing, and thus her privacy would be violated by other people's knowing. "I feel my body, my bones and flesh beginning to open and part upon the alone and the process of coming unalone is terrible," she says (*AILD*, 61–62). Losing a mother at the same time that she is becoming one, Dewey Dell feels an abject need to connect, to communicate with someone who could help her, and an equally abject loneliness in the face of her body's naturally determined fate. Darl's knowledge is not a comfort but a threat; he might reveal what he knows. "Are you going to tell Pa are you going to kill him?" she silently asks him (*AILD*, 27). So she has no one with whom to share either her grief or her fear. "I feel like a wet seed wild in the hot blind earth," she says (*AILD*, 64). Cash and Darl, as we have seen, depend upon sensory and physical reality for their sense of being in the world, but they do not face the threat to individual integrity posed by a body that is growing something on its own, blindly indifferent to the will or consciousness of the self it houses. Dewey Dell, then, literally embodies the state of alienation between self and world that her brothers experience each in his own distinctive way at the loss of their mother. But none of the men in the novel can understand Dewey Dell's situation. Only Addie could understand it and Addie is dead.

But we can better understand Dewey Dell because of what Addie explains about motherhood in her single monologue. After she gives birth to her first child, Cash, Addie says, "I knew that motherhood was invented by someone who had to have a word for it because the ones that had the children didn't care whether there was a word for it or not." Becoming a mother, indeed, founds Addie's most important discovery in the course of a long and difficult life, "that words are no good; that words don't ever fit even what they are trying to say at" (*AILD*, 171–172).

The gap between words and deeds is the novel's central and most inclusive version of the problem its form enunciates—how to connect with others and the larger world and yet remain a self. It is noteworthy that Faulkner ascribes the wisdom to phrase the issue in its most philosophically sophisticated form to a woman. Addie's words assume a privileged status in part, of course, because she is dead—even though she does not yet have a grave to speak "from beyond." But her authority stems more fundamentally from her status as a woman and a mother, and one who sees well beneath the social structure in which she has lived. Faulkner here provides a portrait of female strength and integrity that calls into question the charge of misogyny that his work can so readily invite. Always drawn both toward and away from women, Faulkner here creates one worthy of our respect, if also of our fear. For Addie is a frightening figure, in not only deed but word. Alarmingly articulate, even given her background as a schoolteacher, Addie delivers a brilliant and telling account of what it means to be an individual subject and the family's most essential member at the same time.

When she meets Anse Bundren, Addie is alone in the world. All her family are dead and buried in Jefferson, where she apparently was born. We know nothing about them, except that her father was a sardonic pessimist, telling her that "the reason for living is to get ready to stay dead a long time" (*AILD*, 169). Addie treats this sentence almost as if it were a sentence in the legal sense, a penance she must pay out, or perhaps a kind of curse that she must try to lift by disproving it. On the face of it, the sentence is baffling. Even if one were to accept the claim, how would one "get ready to stay dead," exactly? This is not after all a simple call to pleasure, not a carpe diem. By giving death a temporal measure, the sentence implies a kind of gothic horror, as if one were sentenced not merely to life in prison with no possibility of parole, but to an eternity of still life, *nature morte*. An Edgar Allan Poe would appreciate this line, as it seems to attribute eternal consciousness to a corpse in a box.

As Addie interprets it, however, the sentence provokes a desire to connect directly to life while it is there. She looks forward to whipping the schoolchildren because then at least in the child's "secret and selfish life," she would have "marked" their blood with her own" (*AILD*, 170). Despite his ungainly appearance and uncouth behavior, Addie marries Anse in the hope of making a connection, but childbirth only makes a temporary difference. It is not that Addie doesn't love Cash but rather that her experience has left her again alone, and has taught her that there is no fundamental connection between words and actual deeds, actual physical living. Nor is there a real connection between people, who have "to use one another by words like spiders dangling by their mouths from a beam, swinging and twisting and never touching" (*AILD*, 172). Only by repudiating the word, as it were, by having a secret affair with the minister, the man most empowered by words in her culture, does Addie find a way of connecting herself to someone outside herself. But the connection is not finally with Whitfield, but with Jewel. With his birth "the wild blood boiled away and the sound of it ceased. Then there was only the milk, warm and calm, and I lying calm in the slow silence, getting ready to clean my house" (*AILD*, 176). In part, "cleaning" her house means compensating Anse for any possible loss she may have caused him. She bears Anse two more children, Dewey Dell, "to negative Jewel," and Vardaman, "to replace the child I had robbed him of" (*AILD*, 176). But she also means that she has discovered how to get ready to die. She has come to agree with her father's claim, but, as she puts it, "he could not have known what he meant himself, because a man cannot know anything about cleaning up the house afterward" (*AILD*, 175–176).

To understand Addie's point here, it is useful to recall Dr. Peabody's remark about death: "The nihilists say it is the end; the fundamentalists, the beginning; when in reality it is no more than a single tenant or family moving out of a tenement or a town" (*AILD*, 44). "Cleaning up the house afterward" brings to bear a similar homely and domestic viewpoint on death but understands it from the woman's position within the house, so to speak, rather than from Dr. Peabody's ironic distance. Cleaning up the house entails paying off debts, folding and giving away linens, making sure not to leave behind anything a new "tenant" might find burdensome. It means understanding that the world will still be there for others, and especially your family, to cope with, even though you will be gone. It means knowing you will be gone, which entails knowing that you are, as well as have, a body, and that your relation to the world depends upon that body. She can get ready to die, clean her house, because in bearing children whose blood is not just hers, but the earth's as well, she has connected herself to the "words that are deeds," rather than the words like motherhood "that are just gaps in people's lack" (*AILD*, 174)—which is not to say that she has escaped or transcended the world of words. "Cleaning up the house" acknowledges that world and its demands. And the promise Addie exacts from Anse to bury her in Jefferson underscores her clear understanding that words can be powerful, no matter how much they may fail to fit what they are trying to "say at."

The promise Anse makes to Addie is a telling example of the gap between words and deeds, actually. Addie regards this promise as a means of getting revenge on Anse for his failures as a husband. But Anse's insistence on fulfilling the promise is transparently motivated by his desire to get a set of teeth, at a minimum, a new Mrs. Bundren, at a maximum. He takes the "word" he has given and uses it for his own selfish purposes. On the other hand, the trials and tribulations he must survive in order to meet those purposes are sufficiently gruesome that we might argue that Addie does get her revenge, that word and deed do, ironically, match up. The problem with this view, however, is that it is not Anse who suffers, but his family and neighbors. Anse complains often and loudly of his various burdens, but his complaints only serve to underscore and reinforce his power. As Darl notes, "There is no sweat stain on [Anse's] shirt." "He was sick once from working in the sun when he was twenty-two years old, and he tells people that if he ever sweats, he will die. I suppose he believes it" (*AILD*, 17).

Among the most contemptible characters in Faulkner's fiction, Anse figures forth a vicious satire on fatherhood, much as Addie serves to de-sentimentalize the mother. If her character cuts through the false postures of motherhood that Cora Tull embodies, Anse's character reveals that fatherhood itself is a kind of imposture. Consider that he does no real work. He depends on his children, his neighbors, and the good Lord to take care of him. Although a well-known leech, Anse never misses an opportunity to insist that he and his would not be "beholden" to anyone. He refuses, for example, all offers of food and shelter made along the road to Jefferson, insisting that he and his children will sleep outside or in the barn. What is important to understand about Anse is that he is not actually a hypocrite. Darl is right when he says, "I suppose he believes it." In voicing the position of a self-sufficient yeoman farmer, Anse believes what he says. In that belief he is aided and abetted by those around him, who have helped him out so long and so often that they don't know how not to do it. Thus is Anse sustained in his self-regard, even as he is exposed as dependent on others. Thus affirmed from all sides as what he believes himself to be—an independent and authoritative father—he sees himself accordingly. Anse is always in charge, defying all suggestions that perhaps he ought to bury Addie nearby, given the obstacles to be confronted in taking her to Jefferson. From the novel's outset we see him ordering his family around very effectively, and in the end, thanks to the sacrifice of Jewel's horse, Dewey Dell's money, and Cash's broken leg, Anse gets everything he wants.

Anse is certainly powerful, but his power is revealed as an imposture, a sustained fiction of authority in which all collude. His paternal authority, in other words, is in effect constituted by a collective fiction on which he depends and in which, of course, he believes. His family and friends support Anse in thinking of himself as the father (one always aligned with The Father), even though he is a living contradiction of what a father is supposed to be. His power is real, but grounded in a cultural delusion. Meanwhile, the positive aspects of the father's role—productive agent, protective presence, affectionate supporter—are wholly absent. It seems that as he moved decisively into the role of husband and father himself, Faulkner delivered a radical analysis of the family structure itself.

In *The Sound and the Fury*, Faulkner had represented a family in which a weak and cynical father and a monstrously self-absorbed mother leave their children to grow up in terrible need of authentic and loving parents. In *As I Lay Dying*, we are no longer presented simply with good or bad fathers and mothers but with questions more fundamental. What is a mother? What is a father? What is a family? Further, although the novel affords a certain kind of realistic vision of the rural South in the late 1920s, it does so by formal means that raise the stakes enormously on how much a novel can do, demanding that we consider Addie, for example, not only as an individual character in a story but also as the site of the struggle entailed in being a person as well as a mother, alone and unalone. Further, in foregrounding the gap between words and deeds, the novel brings directly to the surface the issue of language already at work in *The Sound and the Fury*. The possibility that words relate only arbitrarily to their meaning, and thus that our speech is "full of sound and fury, signifying nothing," becomes in *As I Lay Dying* a central hypothesis, one tested explicitly in Addie Bundren's efforts to connect word with deed. In focusing so centrally on the gap between language and reality, the novel calls into question its own validity; after all, the book is made up of words. How are we to regard the relationship between its words and the world it represents?

This issue is particularly foregrounded by the most radical feature of Faulkner's experimental procedure in this novel, his effort to represent the interior experience of semi-literate peasants. A good deal of modernist literature was devoted to finding ways of representing what had hitherto been considered unrepresentable. Joyce, for example, invented the stream of consciousness technique so as to make available, to re-present, the chaotic interior lives we lead, lives that would otherwise remain silent and opaque, and Woolf stretched the possibilities of this technique so as to enrich and expand our understanding of consciousness itself. Faulkner learned from Joyce and Woolf both, but he took the question in a new direction: how do you represent the interiority of people whose socially and economically impoverished lives limit their language to a regional and rural idiom? One can be constrained by such an idiom and still think profoundly, but if the novel remained within the limits of what is sayable for most of its characters, it would not be able to represent the experiences of Vardaman, Dewey Dell, Addie, and especially Darl.

In part, Faulkner uses the same ploy he had used in *The Sound and the Fury* with Benjy. Benjy's retarded mental condition enables us to see the Compson world from a kind of privileged viewpoint, one undistorted by self-consciousness and closely in touch with the sensual experience of the physical environment. Darl's madness does similar work, extending our focus across space and time and bringing to bear an exquisite attention to physical detail. But Benjy's unmediated responses confer on the world that comes into view through his consciousness an indisputable reality; he has no ability or need to interpret, he just reacts, and so we have no reason to doubt him. (Understanding him is another question.) By contrast, Darl's madness inevitably calls into question the relation between his words and the things they are trying to "say at." It is not so much that we don't roughly accept Darl's account of, say, the moment of his mother's death, a scene from which he is absent. (What choice do we have?) It is rather that the language he speaks could not be spoken by a character socially situated as he is. We might accept that language as uniquely the product of Darl's madness, but Faulkner is not content to leave it at that. Other characters speak in similarly lyric ways. Here, for example is Vardaman as he encounters Jewel's horse immediately following his mother's death:

It is as though the dark were resolving him out of his integrity, into an unrelated scattering of components—snuffings and stampings; smells of cooling flesh and ammoniac hair; an illusion of a co-ordinated whole of splotched hide and strong bones within which, detached and secret and familiar, an *is* different from my *is* (*AILD*, 56).

The principle of verisimilitude is not just questioned but obliterated here, as Faulkner deploys in effect an epic simile to represent Vardaman's vision of the horse. But to what end? Faulkner is deliberately dramatizing the gap between words and experience in the conventional realist sense, but in the interest of a more radically committed realism. Words seem to us inadequate most often when our experience is so extreme that "words cannot describe it." At such moments, we particularly feel the need for figurative language, even to approximate what we feel. "It was like X," we say, summoning up a description that draws on analogy, whether to memory or to fantasy. The experience of a seven-year-old in losing his mother is certainly extreme. How to do justice to it then? We need external observation, and Faulkner provides it in abundance. For example, Darl tells us, "From behind Pa's leg Vardaman peers, his mouth full open all color draining from his face into his mouth, as though he has by some means fleshed his own teeth in himself, sucking" (*AILD*, 49). Thanks to Darl, we know that Vardaman is in shock, but Vardaman himself must be enabled to express it if we are to experience its power and its pain.

Such pain, Faulkner is insisting, is not limited to the lives of those educated to express it. On every class level, culture provides us with plenty of tired clichés to defend against death as well as life, as Addie eloquently reminds us. Her husband Anse, for example, thinks, as he speaks, in a wholly clichéd religious vocabulary. But Vardaman has no seamless religious myth within which to wrap himself in his encounter with his mother's departure. Confronted with the prospect of his mother being shut up inside a box, he recalls once being shut up inside the barn crib, where he "couldn't breathe because the rat was breathing up all the air" (*AILD*, 66). Consequently, he drills holes in the coffin so his mother can breathe. On the other hand, since his mother is obviously not there, in some profound sense, Vardaman opines that she has become a fish, and hopes that she has escaped the coffin and swum into the river when the wagon turns over in it. Literal thinking here is also magical thinking. Given Vardaman's imaginative powers and the desperation that fuels them, his description of the horse seems not so improbable after all. He may lack the vocabulary invoked here, but he does not lack a grasp of what he is experiencing—an "is different from my is," a body that is alien to his. The brilliant metaphorical description here is born of terror and signals an unjustly accelerated introduction to being separate and alone.

Such language, then, serves both to illustrate and extend Addie's point about the inadequacy of conventional language. Like "motherhood," the language of grief has long since become a "gap to fill a lack," blocking what it should open up, a connection between word and deed. The novel's perverse version of the Bundrens' funeral procession itself opens up the aching void between the ossified social rituals of mourning and the actual experience of loss they are supposed to inform with meaning. If the novel is to reopen the circuit between word and deed, it must outstrip the limits of verisimilitude, itself an artificial convention designed to simulate, rather than re-present, the real. Accordingly, when we find Darl, Vardaman, and Dewey Dell speaking in extravagently figurative language, what we would ordinarily call "raw" experience assumes the form of words that are, almost, deeds. Indeed, in voicing these characters' emotional and psychic distress, the novel is engaged in the struggle that Addie describes—the struggle to make words into deeds.

Like his fellow modernists, Faulkner was trying to reinvent the novel, and like the greatest of them, he sought help from the Greek epic. In this case, he seems to have found a particularly rich resource in *The Odyssey*. When Odysseus summons forth the dead for conversation in Book XI, many of them have been dead "a long time," but thanks to the ritual he carries out, he can enable them to speak to him. The ritual makes possible communication between the son and the mother, the living and the dead, much as the epic convention of the *nekuia*, the visiting of the dead, enables Homer to represent that communication and the human bonds it both reveals and secures. In *As I Lay Dying*, Faulkner uses another ritual designed to relate the living to the dead, the funeral, to portray the gap between what it should make possible and what it actually reveals—the alienation not only of the living from the dead but of the living from the living as well. Formally, in both its multiple mono-logues and in the range of voices and idioms it summons forth, the novel seeks to cross the gaps it represents.

In 1957, a student at the University of Virginia asked Faulkner about the similarities between *As I Lay Dying* and Nathaniel Hawthorne's *The Scarlet Letter*, both of which tell the story of a minister's adulterous relation to a woman. Hester Prynne's illegitimate child is named Pearl, Addie Bundren's is named Jewel, and the Reverend Whitfield's name seems a deliberate play on the Reverend Dimmesdale's. Faulkner's response is among his most telling, and deserves full quotation:

> No, a writer don't have to consciously parallel because he robs and steals from everything he ever wrote or read or saw. I was simply writing a *tour de force* and as every writer does, I took whatever I needed wherever I could find it, without any compunction and with no sense of violating any ethics or hurting anyone's feelings because any writer feels that anyone after him is perfectly welcome to take any trick he has learned or any plot that he has used. Of course we don't know just who Hawthorne took his from. Which he probably did because there are so few plots to write about. (*University*, 115)

A whole theory of literature is implied here, one in which the artist's originality is ironically affirmed in the very act of bragging that as an artist, he belongs to a company of thieves. Faulkner was keenly aware of how thoroughly enmeshed his imagination was with literature from the Greeks to the Romantics. (He carried a one-volume Shakespeare around with him and read *Don Quixote* once a year.) As a novelist, however, he enjoyed the company of his predecessors rather than fearing any dependency on them. In leaving poetry behind, that is, he had discarded, or at least deferred, the "anxiety of influence," as Harold Bloom has designated the modern writer's oedipal struggle with his literary fathers.[8] It is possible that Faulkner saw the parallels between his characters' situation and that of Hawthorne's emerging only in the course of composition and decided it would be entertaining to allude to Dimmesdale and Pearl, offering his reader a kind of amusing inside joke.

As for plots, meanwhile, Faulkner knew them to be, formally speaking, limited in both number and potential. In his next novel, he exhibits a certain impatience with such limits by piling plot upon plot.

It would take a long literary survey to identify the sources from which Faulkner might have robbed his plots for *Light in August*, his next novel, but of more interest is how many of them there are. There is the story of Joe Christmas. There is the story of Lena Grove, of Gail Hightower, of Byron Bunch and Joanna Burden, just to name the leading figures in the novel's capacious drama. As he expands the scope of his fiction from the family to the town, Faulkner persists in his ongoing experimentation with narrative. Here, our disorientation derives less from the use of multiple perspectives than from the multiplicity of plot lines. Each story necessitates another, until plot lines seem to spread out indefinitely. As he did in *As I Lay Dying*, Faulkner refuses us a single, fixed perspective, but not by placing us in several minds successively; rather, he moves us from one place and time to another as the narrator focuses his attention on one character's story only to turn away to another's, as if he too were trying to keep up with the stories he's trying to tell.

The novel's opening three chapters both illustrate and initiate this process. At the end of the first chapter, Faulkner turns from Lena, now in sight of Jefferson, to Byron Bunch's memories of Joe Christmas's arrival in Jefferson in the second chapter. Not until we are several pages into the chapter do we meet Brown, the man whom we would expect the author to introduce in the next episode of a book which, so far, seems to be centrally concerned with Lena Grove. So while confusion between Bunch and Burch leads Lena to expect Burch to be at the mill when she arrives, the reader, for the same reason, expects a comic plot to develop. Instead, we are introduced to a new character, Joe Christmas, whose story seems utterly irrelevant. By virtue of his name and his ominous affect, however, Joe Christmas cannot be a minor character, so we adjust our expectations to encompass the possibility of tragedy, only to meet in the third chapter still another character, Gail Hightower, whose relationship to Lena and Christmas must now be established somehow. From the outset, in short, the novel disrupts any expectations of a single or unified plot structure.

The opening pages of *Light in August* locate us in a world in motion, drawing us not, as in *The Sound and the Fury*, into a present scene whose meaning is fleshed out fully once we learn its relationship to the past, but rather into a moving present capable of leading us virtually anywhere. Lena Grove's quest to find the father of her unborn child, precisely by virtue of its apparent hopelessness, promises to carry us on an endless journey. The novel that proceeds from this beginning makes good on this promise; its plots proliferate at an alarming rate. But while forcing us to attend to the question of what will happen next in a present always moving forward, Faulkner also meets the demand that grows more urgent as this present grows more complex, the demand to fill in the history of the characters whose actions we witness. Our need as readers to explain present events by reference to their history, therefore, coexists—by no means peacefully—with our need to keep up with them as they pull us forward into an indeterminate future. The narrative pulls us, in other words, in two directions at once, forward into the future and backward into the past. Accordingly, as the novel moves forward through the three weeks that constitute its present, it must also move backward into the past to fill in the stories of its proliferating characters.

The opening chapter deploys a brilliant mechanism for moving the reader into the ongoing motion of the novel. As Lena sits beside the road watching Armstid's wagon approach, Faulkner describes the scene in terms of a contradiction between what she sees and what she hears.

> The sharp and brittle crack and clatter of its weathered and ungreased wood and metal is slow and terrific: a series of dry sluggish reports carrying for a half mile across the hot still pinewiney silence of the August afternoon. Though the mules plod in a steady and unflagging hypnosis, the vehicle does not seem to progress. It seems to hang suspended in the middle distance forever and forever, so infinitesimal is its progress.[9]

What Faulkner produces here is the impression of constant motion. The wagon's sound signals its motion, "slow and terrific," while its appearance is static, "suspended . . . forever and forever." He is appealing to our predisposition to view immobility as a sign of permanence, but complicating our responses by attributing that permanence to motion itself. The wagon is moving, but "does not seem to progress," and Lena's own relation to time is similar.

> she advanced in identical and anonymous and deliberate wagons as though through a succession of creakwheeled and limpeared avatars, like something moving forever and without progress across an urn (*LIA*, 7).

Faulkner's invocation of Keats's Grecian urn underscores Lena's pastoral habitation of the natural, procreative realm from which, as we will learn, Joe Christmas is alienated and

Gail Hightower has fled. But Lena also inhabits and represents a world in steady motion, time moving inexorably onward. "My my," she remarks, "a body does get around" (*LIA*, 30).

Even so young and uncomplex a character as Lena has a past, which must be adduced for us to understand her. The novel's second paragraph, thus, begins a roughly three-page flashback providing the story of where she has come from and why. When she thinks *"I am now further from Doane's Mill than I have been since I was twelve years old,"* it is as if the narrator hears her, and steps in to explain. "She had never been to Doane's Mill until after her father and mother died" (*LIA*, 3). The story is quickly told, and it is a bleak one. Lena lost both her parents at twelve, and moved to Doane's Mill to live with her much older brother and his habitually pregnant wife. She eventually began crawling out the window of her lean-to room to meet Lucas Burch, who disappeared as soon as he learned she was pregnant. She has been walking for four weeks in quest of him, hitching rides on wagons from country folk who have never heard of Lucas Burch but are unwilling to discourage her. Once this background is filled in, we return to Lena sitting on the road, and time moves forward again. But it is important to note that Faulkner has enfolded into this short flashback a remarkable paragraph in which the history of Doane's Mill itself is presented.

The narrator draws back from the immediate past to position himself as if he were omniscient, at least insofar as he is endowed with the ability to see the future as well as the past. The lumber mill "had been there seven years and in seven years more it would destroy all the timber within its reach." Then most of the machinery and the men who "existed because of and for it" would gradually disappear, leaving a "stumppocked scene of profound and peaceful desolation" (*LIA*, 4–5). It is as if a camera had filmed a fourteen-year sequence, which we are seeing projected in fast-forward mode. But the projectionist here is by no means neutral in his aims. The destruction wrought by the lumber industry, its ruthless exploitation of both men and nature, is recounted in vivid detail. The simple flashback designed to provide us with Lena's life story so far doubles as a vehicle for situating that story within a dramatically larger one, filling out a picture of the socioeconomic world from which all the Lenas and the Burches have emerged.

This strategy is writ large in the novel as a whole. As the novel's present flows on into an indeterminate future, we move simultaneously farther and farther into the past until, with Hightower's reveries in Chapter 20, we reach a point before the civil war. The novel appropriates larger and larger chunks of time into a structure that is constantly struggling to enfold them within a unified vision. The novel not only operates on this principle but calls attention to it by deliberately, as it were, biting off more than it seems able to chew. As time moves on and plots multiply and crosshatch with each other, the novel sets itself an enormous task of assimilation; as the structure expands to encompass a lengthening history within an ordered whole, that order is continually revealing itself as inadequate to the larger demands for meaning posed by the continuously moving present. Thus the tension keeps mounting between time's ceaseless motion and the need to impose a structure large enough to give that motion meaning. Hightower's vision offers the novel's final and most ambitious effort to achieve a redemptive understanding of the human community as it has been dramatized in the novel's interlocking plots, but it does not cohere. Faulkner further emphasizes the inadequacy of any redeeming vision by ending the novel as he does, not with Hightower, but with Lena.

It is as if a whole new story is about to begin. A new character, the furniture salesman, is introduced to relate to his wife the story of Byron and Lena as they leave Jefferson for an unknown future. The story he tells is basically a humorous one, mildly making fun of Byron for his subordination to Lena, and thus provides a kind of comic relief to the horrifying drama we have just witnessed. Having entered the novel with Lena, we exit it with her as well. But Lena's story acts not only as bracket but also as ellipsis; it encloses and relieves the tragedy of Joe Christmas, but it also extends and amplifies its intensity. Lena is in many obvious ways an admirable character, and the story of her rescue by Byron is heartening in its revelation of his strength and her simple faith in the power of nature. But it is worth recalling that the single time her story overlaps directly with that of Joe Christmas, she is thrown into confusion. When Mrs. Hines wants to name her child Joe, Lena gets "mixed up." "I don't like to get mixed up," Lena says, insisting that she has not named the child yet (*LIA*, 410). Lena's resistance to getting mixed up here is significant in several ways, but among them is that it underscores the fundamental boundary dividing her world from Joe's. She knows her child will need a name, and not only a first one, but she effectively asserts the right to choose it. Given her situation, Lena has remarkable power, but the definitive distance she maintains from Joe's world signals the limits of her story as a resource for redeeming his. Her story provides, in other words, a way of getting "out of the novel," but it insistently fails to meet the need for closure it ostensibly fulfills. That need is rendered acute by the novel's central story—that of Joe Christmas. Before turning to it, we need to stand back for a moment to recognize the radical nature of Faulkner's experiment here.

The novel enacts a struggle for form, one that will unify its plots and thereby endow human time with meaning. As always, Faulkner was trying to put it all "between one Cap and one period" (*FCF*, 14). But his narrative strategy in this novel moves beyond that of his earlier work not only in formal terms, but in its dramatic, sometimes explosive expansion into the social and political dimensions of Yoknapatawpha. As we have seen with Lena in Chapter 1, the pressure to backtrack and give a character a past leads the narrator to expand his focus, providing a social context for that character's experience. We soon learn that the more complex the character, the more of a history we need, and thus the more of a context. So when Joe Christmas takes center stage, the narrator devotes eight chapters to the task that took four pages with Lena Grove. Like Lena's story, Joe's is bleak, but unlike Lena's it is profoundly tragic, and in the course of telling it, as he did with Lena, the narrator takes us not only into Joe's personal experience but into the social, religious, and racialized world that forms it.

The story of Joe Christmas as it unfolds from Chapters 5 through 12 virtually constitutes a novel within a novel, a *bildungsroman* in which the protagonist's education and growth to maturity make him an alien to all the worlds through which he moves. At each site of his progress from infant to grown man, his alienation is reconfirmed, spurring on the gathering threat his existence poses to the world and the world poses to his survival, the threat that is finally realized in his murder of Joanna

Burden and the town's lynching of him. At the core of this threat is Joe's racial identity, or rather, his lack of one. Called "nigger" as a child at the orphanage, he has no way of understanding that label until the dietitian uses it in upbraiding him when she finds him hiding in her closet. Wrongly assuming Joe has understood the sexual act taking place beyond the closet curtain, the dietitian first tries to bribe him to keep him from telling on her. Joe fails to understand the bribe, leading the dietitian to conclude that he plans to tell what happened. She then maneuvers his removal from the orphanage by convincing the matron that he is black. Thus for Joe, the "woman-smelling" closet is tied to the word "nigger," an identification of race and sex that will finally issue in the novel's most telling verbal invention, "womanshenegro" (*LIA*, 120,121). Eventually, Joe is adopted by the McEacherns, who know nothing of his past. But by that time, at age five, Joe already knows his shameful secret—as he later puts it, he has "some nigger blood" in him, a belief already bound up with his fear of women (*LIA*, 196). Joe develops an obsessively masculine identity enacted through his stoic and finally violent defiance of his father, but more fundamentally grounded in his rejection of his mother, "the woman: that soft kindness which he believed himself doomed to be forever victim of and which he hated worse than he did the hard and ruthless justice of men" (*LIA*, 168–169).

When Joe shows up in Jefferson at the age of thirty-three, he has fully internalized the opposition between black and white, so that his identity is secured precisely by that opposition, although the security it affords is fragile at best, explosive at worst. When he sleeps with white prostitutes whom he lacks the money to pay, he announces afterward that he is black and they kick him out in a rage. He has learned how to manipulate the society's racism, one might say. But when he tries this tactic in a more northern city, the prostitute is unphased. "What about it?" she says. "You look all right" (*LIA*, 225). Joe beats her almost to death. He cannot tolerate the possibility that the racial line might not matter, as in that case he has no identity at all. He tricks white men into calling him black "in order to fight them," and in turn, when Negroes call him white, he fights them (*LIA*, 225). What is constant is Joe's antagonistic relation to both black and white. If he chooses one over the other, he cannot survive the threat to his singular identity, founded as it is in defiance of *both* black and white. Joe carries within himself, as a physical as well as a cultural burden, the fundamental racism of his society.

It is important to understand that for the racist culture on display here, "black versus white" is not just a distinction between two kinds of people. It is what some cultural theorists call a binary opposition. That is, each term means the negation of the other: black means not white; white means not black. As Joe Christmas's physical appearance indicates, these terms do not necessarily refer to skin color per se. As it functions socially in the world of Faulkner's novel, this opposition is most fully expressed as white man versus "nigger." When the marshal, for example, hears Lucas Burch call Joe Christmas a "nigger," he replies, "You better be careful what you are saying, if it is a white man you are talking about . . . . I don't care if he is a murderer or not" (*LIA*, 98). The virulence of basic racial opposition here outstrips the force of almost all other distinctions, including murderer/not murderer. When the southerner Quentin Compson decides that "nigger is not a person so much as a form of behavior; a sort of obverse reflection of the white people he lives among," he is implicitly acknowledging the interdependency of the two terms (*S&F*, 55). His perspective is indisputably racist, but he has at least gotten beyond the lawyer Gavin Stevens in *Light in August*, for whom "nigger" has taken on the reified status accorded it by the language of "blood." He undertakes to explain Joe Christmas's erratic behavior by reference to the "black blood which snatched up the pistol and the white blood which would not let him fire it" (*LIA*, 449). The townspeople as well resort to the idiom of blood: "He don't look any more like a nigger than I do. But it must have been the nigger blood in him," one man says. (*LIA*, 349). The same man later admits that he is stumped by Joe: "He never acted like either a nigger or a white man. . . . That was what made the folks so mad" (*LIA*, 350). The opposition is, as it has been from the novel's outset, exposed as wholly irrational. But if Joe is neither a "nigger" nor a "white man," what is he? In this culture, he has no place to be, save in combat with the opposition that constitutes him. Faulkner explodes the "blood" myth by which the tragic mulatto figure in American literary and cultural history is trapped: the idea that people of mixed racial descent are part black, part white, and forced therefore to choose whether or not to "pass." Whichever choice they make, they reaffirm the binary opposition that condemns them to the choice in the first place. Joe Christmas refuses to make that choice; he refuses to "pass" on a sustained basis, and he refuses to live as a "nigger," not least because he has been brought up not only as white but as a racist.

Joe's life also centers on the line dividing male from female, another binary opposition of incalculable force in this novel.

As with the race line that constitutes and divides him at once, the gender line defines him as an arch-masculine figure, terrified at any encroachment by the slippery and unpredictable behavior of women, from the dietitian to Bobbie, and finally even to Joanna, once she has quit behaving like a man and started praying over him. Joe has been well-schooled in what it means to be "a man," an identity at once fully embodied by McEachern and thoroughly inflicted on Joe as he grows up. The depth of this ingrained masculine identity is confirmed when he listens to Joanna tell the story of her grandfather and her brother being killed by Colonel Sartoris. He asks her why her father didn't kill Sartoris in revenge, and Joanna responds, "You would have. Wouldn't you?" "'Yes,' he said at once, immediately." When Joanna speculates that it was "because of his French blood" that her father didn't kill Sartoris, Joe replies, "Don't even Frenchmen get mad when a man kills his father and his son on the same day?" (*LIA*, 245–254).

Joe's alignment with a masculine code of blood revenge may seem odd, given his own lack of a family line like that of the Burdens, not to mention his own violent relations with his father. But his attitude reflects his deep absorption into the ideologies demanded by the gender system and on display throughout the novel. We have noted Faulkner's own struggles with masculine codes of identity, and here we find him exploring their sources and consequences with a ferocity hitherto unseen in his work. What he finds is that the gender system dictates that men act, and act violently, not just when necessary but whenever possible. As an extreme example of the society's model of masculinity, Joe's attitudes and behavior reveal violence as the core of male identity. The novel is replete with scenes and stories of men's addiction to violence. In this respect it is crucial for Byron Bunch to fight Lucas Burch, even though he knows he will lose, because otherwise he will not have the male credentials to become Lena's husband. What is the reason, if any, for this masculine need for violence? Joe's story offers one explanation of its source.

When Joe tries to lose his virginity, going out with his friends for a prearranged rural assignation with a young black girl, Joe's fear of women is fused and confused with his self-identification as Negro. Filled with a "terrible haste" and remembering "toothpaste," Joe looks down upon the girl and sees himself; he seems "to look down into a black well," at the bottom of which are "two glints like reflections of black stars" (*LIA*, 156). Reenacted in racial terms, this portrayal of Narcissus, which Faulkner had repeatedly written about during his poetic apprenticeship, reveals Joe's deep identification with the black as woman, the woman as black. The sexual desire she provokes instantly turns to rage at the threat that connection with her inspires. Viciously attacking her, Joe enacts his first, but determining and lifelong, rebellion against the "womanshenegro," who is basically himself in female form. His internalized racial self-hatred finds an external target in the same female body designated as the object of his heterosexual desire. The racial issue enables Faulkner to represent the terror of women as a major source of male violence. Faulkner does not set Joe apart as a deviant, but uses the outcast—as he does throughout this novel—to reveal the core of the cultural systems on which the society depends for its coherence, as well as its incoherence.

Race and gender systems are so intertwined in the culture into which Joe is initiated that they cannot be fully disentangled, but it is important to recognize the force with which the novel addresses gender and sexuality as major cultural predicates for imposing and enforcing power relations just as fiercely as the racial system does. In this culture, women suffer, smell out sin if they're good and indulge in it if they're not, and connive in secrecy against their male husbands and fathers. The imperviousness with which Lena Grove—a walking outrage to the good women—negotiates her way through and around the strictures of marriage and legitimacy only serves to highlight the dehumanizing effects of those strictures. The cost to women of the Protestant culture's repression of female sexuality is made painfully evident in Joanna Burden's brief escape from it. In addition to dramatizing the depth of the southern white woman's sexual repression—by means of describing graphically what happens when that repression is lifted—Faulkner's account of the Joe/Joanna episode underscores the major role played by religion in sustaining racist norms. The sexual politics of southern racism are clear enough. Joanna whispers "Negro, negro negro" as she makes love to Joe, seduced by the very image that haunts the southern white men who fear the black man's sexual power (*LIA*, 260). But at least as important to the larger vision of race hatred that the novel anatomizes is the religious faith on which that race hatred feeds. Although the racism that Faulkner is so virulently attacking in this novel is clearly the central object of its thematic focus, we cannot properly appreciate that attack without understanding religion's role as the major agent and resource of racial hatred in the culture under scrutiny.

Thus, Gail Hightower's story becomes crucial, even if at the outset it seems far off center. Through Hightower, we get a privileged picture of the church, privileged by virtue of his being an outcast from it. In Hightower's final reverie, the church is described as a failure not because of the "outward groping of those within it nor the inward groping of those without," but because of the "professionals who control it and who have removed the bells from its steeples." Having effectively castrated the church's power to provide any meaningful order for time's onward movement, the professionals have left only the steeples, "endless without order, empty, symbolical, bleak, skypointed not with ecstasy or passion but in adjuration, threat and doom" (*LIA*, 487). What Hightower's vision reveals is that the people of Jefferson form a community devoted not to fostering life, the "treble shouts of generations," but rather to death, an attitude demonstrated by that "Protestant music" with its "quality stern and implacable, deliberate and without passion so much as immolation, pleading, asking, for not love, not life, forbidding it to others, demanding in sonorous tones death as though death were the boon" (*LIA*, 367).

Light in August is an angry novel, angry at the people who succumb to the comforts of hatred and the titillations of violence. In the opening pages of Chapter 13 we return to the scene of Joanna's death and the descent upon her house of the townspeople: they "knew, believed, and hoped that she had been ravished too: at least once before her throat was cut and at least once afterward" (*LIA*, 288). They immediately begin "to canvass about for someone to crucify" (*LIA*, 289). As for Percy Grimm, the self-appointed agent of their vengeance, Faulkner was later to brag that he had "created a Nazi before Hitler did."[10] As the novel unfolds, the expanding social and historical terrain it opens up breeds ever new opportunities for outrage and despair. The narrator's anger and contempt sometimes threatens to disrupt the novel's rhythmic flashes between present and past. In Chapter 13, for example, his tirade continues beyond a description of the scene to an indictment of the people's refusal "to forgive her and let her be dead in peace and quiet" because their violent fantasies of rape and murder "made nice believing" (*LIA*, 289). The narrator's rage extends the passage from shopkeepers to lawyers, doctors, women. You realize at a certain point that he could go on and on, so infuriated is he at the spiritual poverty informing the hunger for violence at the heart of the society he is portraying.

Such outbursts erupt frequently in this novel, testing again its capacity formally to contain the rhetorical energies unleashed by Faulkner's ambitious effort to take on the social world in full force. They also signal the odd position of the novel's narrator. On the one hand, he seems to occupy the omniscient narrator's stance; as we have noticed, he can move in for close-ups and out for panoramic views, collapsing or expanding time and space at will. On the other hand, his knowledge is limited to some extent, since he so often indicates that he is guessing. When Joe pursues Bobbie, he begins to steal money from his mother's hiding place. "It is very possible," the narrator tells us, "that the woman did not suggest it to him, never mentioned money to him." Indeed, "it is possible that he did not even know that he was paying with money for pleasure" (*LIA*, 191). The narrator here prominently displays the limits of his own knowledge, not only as to what Joe knows or doesn't know but also as to what Bobbie did or didn't do. How does the narrator know all that he seems to, and yet have to speculate about even the specific events of the plot whose story he is telling? The answer, I think, is that Faulkner wants to mark the boundaries within which even an omniscient narrator operates. Faulkner must have the services of an omniscient narrator to address the immense breadth and depth of the social space of this novel, but that narrator himself must be understood as searching out the different plot lines as they unfold, imagining one while refusing to give up on an alternate one, as here. He comments at one point that "man knows so little about his fellows" (*LIA*, 47–48). In a novel where what people think they know is often just as suspect as what they believe, the narrator must remind us from time to time that what he knows—despite its magnitude—is not certain or secure. One might put the same point more directly by saying that Faulkner is tipping his hand, showing us that he is making up this story, and in the process making choices while imagining others. As in his earlier ironic self-description for *Forum*, the storyteller is marking both his distance and his vulnerability.

Light in August was a critical turning point in Faulkner's writing career. Not only did he address the issue of race directly for the first time, but he turned decisively toward the broad-based representation of social structures and practices that would occupy him for the rest of his career. The works that had brought him forward into critical acclaim, *The Sound and the Fury* and *As I Lay Dying*, are by no means cut off from social reality, but they approach it from a more insulated, psychologically focused, and formally self-referential vantage point than that at work in *Light in August*. One mark of this shift is the move from a single, nuclear family as the focalizing subject of the story to an array of families, both present and past, set within a densely textured culture whose central axis is the town of Jefferson at the heart of the county called Yoknapatawpha. Families continue to play a dominant role in Faulkner's ongoing representation of this rich social terrain, but they now come with, and are often overcome by, genealogies.

Three

THE MAJOR PHASE, PART 2:
ABSALOM, ABSALOM! AND *GO*
DOWN, MOSES

ONCE *LIGHT IN AUGUST* WAS COMPLETED, FAULKNER FOUND himself in financial trouble again. He had received virtually no royalties from *Sanctuary*, since Hal Smith's fledgling publishing firm went bankrupt. His short story sales were slim and largely unremunerative, and so he accepted an offer from Hollywood, arriving in Culver City, California, at the MGM studios on May 7, 1932. He had a six-week contract at $500.00 a week. It would prove to be the first of many, eventually fairly regular, trips to Hollywood over the next decade, as Faulkner struggled to make enough money to support his family, restore Rowan Oak, and meet his often expensive tastes, not to mention Estelle's. The stories about Faulkner in Hollywood are legion, but in some ways the best come from this first visit. Here are two.

When Faulkner arrived at Sam Marx's office late that Saturday in May, he asked to be assigned either to Mickey Mouse movies, or to newsreels, "the only pictures I like," he explained (Minter, 139). Mickey Mouse movies, Marx explained, were made by the Walt Disney Studio, not MGM. In any case, Faulkner had already been assigned to a film to be called *Flesh*, featuring Wallace Beery, who had recently scored a hit with *The Champ*. Faulkner was sent off to watch the latter film but asked the projectionist to stop it almost immediately, as it was obvious how the story was going to come out. Faulkner then disappeared for ten days, allegedly to Death Valley but certainly into some alcohol-induced haze.

The second story concerns Howard Hawks and Clark Gable. After going nowhere with the various assignments at MGM, Faulkner had been sought out by Howard Hawks to write the screenplay for a story of his own, "Turn About," a project that proved a success. It was made into the film *Today We Live*, starring Joan Crawford. Hawks and Faulkner became good friends; indeed, in the course of his years in Hollywood, most of Faulkner's best work would be done with Hawks, who shared his values as well as his interest in drinking and hunting. It was while on a hunting trip with Hawks and some of his friends, including Clark Gable, that Faulkner delivered a punch line that became famous. Faulkner and Hawks were talking about books, as they drove out of town that day, and Gable, not much of a reader, shyly asked after a while, "Mr. Faulkner, what do you think somebody should read if he wants to read the best modern books?" Faulkner replied with a list of names: "Ernest Hemingway, Willa Cather, Thomas Mann, John Dos Passos, and myself." "Oh," Gable said, "Do you write?" "Yes, Mr. Gable," Faulkner replied, "What do you do?" (Blotner, 310).

Though notoriously shy and silent, obviously Faulkner could participate with wit and bite when moved to do so. He made several friends in Hollywood, and although he never liked it, he wrote a lot and meanwhile learned a good deal about scripts and moviemaking there. To what extent this experience taught him anything he didn't already know about composing a narrative is hard to determine; he had already clearly learned things from watching films, amply demonstrated by his use of flashbacks and zooming in and out in *Light in August*. We do know that Hawks liked to have Faulkner on the set, to patch up scenes and rewrite awkward dialogue when necessary, tasks he was good at and apparently enjoyed performing, especially when working with Humphrey Bogart and Lauren Becall on the set of *The Big Sleep*. But most of the time when Faulkner was in Hollywood over the next decade and more, he wanted to be back in Oxford. Typically, he would leave as soon as he had made enough money to last a while, returning when he ran out. Throughout these years, he kept hoping to sell enough short stories not to have to return to California, but he could never achieve that goal.

In the summer and fall of 1932, Faulkner was not only having trouble learning the screenwriting business, but he was also having trouble writing his own fiction. Partly, of course, this lapse was caused by having to spend time writing for the screen, but partly it was the fatigue bound to follow the period of prodigious productivity through which he had just come. In four years he had published four novels: *The Sound and the Fury, As I Lay Dying, Sanctuary,* and *Light in August,* in addition to several short stories. The following year found him looking after Estelle, pregnant with Jill and in frail condition, and writing a few short stories while still working long distance on another project with Hawks. Although he sold the film rights to *Sanctuary,* and therefore was solvent for a while,

Faulkner found himself unable to produce. The birth of Jill in June 1933 raised spirits and renewed hopes for his marriage, but Faulkner was growing despondent about his career. In October 1933, he wrote Hal Smith, "It has been almost 16 months since I have written anything original."[1] Shortly thereafter, however, he sold a new story, "A Bear Hunt," to the *Saturday Evening Post*, and the following February 1934, he began to work on a new manuscript that would become *Absalom, Absalom!*

Faulkner wrote his publisher that he hoped to complete the novel by the following fall. In the end it took him more than two-and-one-half years to write *Absalom, Absalom!* But unlike the previous two years, this was a period of almost miraculous productivity in Faulkner's career as a writer. While at work on the novel, he published a collection of short stories, *Dr. Martino and Other Stories,* another novel, *Pylon,* as well as writing most of the stories that would make up *The Unvanquished*, published in 1939. During the same period, he also worked on at least four film scripts, *Sutter's Gold, The Road to Glory, Banjo on My Knee,* and *Gunga Din.* What impeded his progress on *Absalom, Absalom!* was in part the immensity of the narrative challenge it posed and in part the intensity of the personal demands he faced during these years. Among the latter, certainly the most significant was his younger brother Dean's death, in an airplane Faulkner had given him, in November 1935. As for the former, the manuscript evidence confirms what Faulkner reported when he set the novel aside in August 1934 after months of work—that he had a "mass of stuff" but no satisfactory way of putting it together yet (*SL*, 84). He turned to *Pylon,* a story of the barnstorming fliers he had come to know since learning to fly and helping set his brother Dean up in business as a pilot in northern Mississippi. Once *Pylon* was published in February 1935, Faulkner turned again to *Absalom, Absalom!* whose structural problems he was now able to solve, thanks, in part perhaps, to the fundamental distance from *Absalom, Absalom!* that its modern and urban subject provided. When he finished the manuscript in January 1936, he was in Hollywood. He gave it to a fellow screenwriter to read, saying, "I think it's the best novel yet written by an American" (Blotner, 364). One could certainly argue that he was right.

With *Absalom, Absalom!* Faulkner returns to his great-grandfather's legend, but with a critical edge that was lacking in *Sartoris*. The nostalgia for the lost world of the heroic fathers, already debunked in *Light in August* in Hightower's final realization that his ancestor's heroic deed was nothing more than a chicken coop raid, is now forsworn for a thoroughgoing interrogation of southern patriarchy, both its foundations and its legacy. On the side, so to speak, Faulkner was writing stories for *The Saturday Evening Post* which would eventually constitute *The Unvanquished* (1939), where the old Bayard Sartoris of his earlier novel returns as a little boy living with his grandmother and his best friend Ringo, a black child with whom he is growing up on the Sartoris plantation. Perhaps this alternate exercise in relating the adventures of Bayard and Ringo helped siphon off any residual romanticism Faulkner may have harbored about the Old South, currently in vogue thanks to the publication of *Gone with the Wind* (1936). In any case, the world of *Absalom, Absalom!* bears very little resemblance to that of *The Unvanquished*. Originally called "Dark House," the novel opens and closes in the dark, and its vision is entirely tragic.

As in the novels we have already discussed, *Absalom, Absalom!* can seem to its first-time reader perversely designed to keep the story from getting itself told. Faulkner provides a Chronology, a Genealogy, and a map of Yoknapatawpha County, but while helpful, these additions by no means answer the key questions raised in the text itself. Who was Thomas Sutpen? Where did he come from? Why did he build his house and plantation? Why did his son Henry kill Charles Bon, Judith's suitor? What happened to Henry? Why is Rosa Coldfield in a rage at Sutpen? It is crucial to recognize, if we are to appreciate this novel, that we are not alone in asking these and other questions. The characters are trying to answer them as well. That's why they are engaged in conversations with each other.

In fact, the novel is built largely of conversations, three of which are dominant—the conversations between Quentin and Rosa, between Quentin and his father, and between Quentin and Shreve. Each conversation can be seen as producing a version of the Sutpen story. The first and in some ways simplest version is Rosa's. In her eyes, Sutpen is a demon, a man who came from nowhere, descended on the town, took her sister in marriage and spawned two demon children. He forbade his daughter's marriage to Charles Bon for no reason, set Henry to kill Bon for no reason, and then committed the ultimate crime in proposing to her that they breed, and if the child turned out to be male, he would marry her. He is, indeed, the devil incarnate, smelling of sulfur, and it is because of him that the South lost the war, since only then could he be punished. Rosa's account raises more questions than it answers, to put it mildly, but it serves admirably to fix Sutpen in our minds as larger than life. The second version is Mr. Compson's. Classically educated and cynically inclined, he explains that Sutpen repudiated his daughter's marriage to Bon because Bon had an octoroon mistress in New Orleans. Henry, according to this account, cannot tolerate the bigamy he sees coming with Bon's marriage to Judith and kills Bon to prevent it. Identifying with Bon as a sophisticated and cosmopolitan figure, Mr. Compson brings him alive but cannot even persuade himself that he has explained Henry's murder of Bon. As he says to Quentin, "It's just incredible. It just does not explain. . . . They are there, yet something is missing; they are like a chemical formula . . . you bring them together in the proportions called for, but nothing happens."[2] Cued in part by Mr. Compson's interest in the love triangle between Judith, Henry, and Bon, Quentin and Shreve then come up with the third and final version of the story, casting Bon and Henry as half-brothers and thereby explaining not only Henry's murder of Bon, but Sutpen's motives for denying his suit as well. If Bon is understood to be Sutpen's oldest son, born in Haiti of a wife Sutpen later discovers is part black, then his arrival at Sutpen's door as Judith's suitor threatens not just incest, which Henry is willing to tolerate, but miscegenation, which he is not. Thus for Shreve and Quentin, the story's climax is reached in the conversation they imagine between Henry and Bon: "You are my brother," Henry says. "No, I'm not," Bon replies, "I'm the nigger that's going to sleep with your sister. Unless you stop me, Henry" (AA, 286). The third and final version of the story is by far the most powerful and convincing, and it is clearly expected to outstrip, incorporate, and supersede the first two—this even though it is the furthest removed in time and the least connected to any empirical evidence.

Although it is useful to identify these three versions of the story, it is also misleading to read the novel primarily by reference to them. To do so is to approach *Absalom, Absalom!* as if it were structured on the same principles as *The Sound and the Fury*. As we have seen, Faulkner was already concerned in his earlier work with his reader and the means by which that reader could be led forward into the past; but in *Absalom, Absalom!* he brings that reader into the dialogue more urgently, compelling him or her to participate directly in the novel's central form of activity—storytelling. In conventional terms, we could say that the reader becomes a narrator, and because the major line of action in the novel's present consists in narration, the reader is threatened with becoming a character. But it is more accurate, I think, to say that the novel is itself a set of voices in dialogue with the reader, who, like Quentin Compson, struggles in vain to secure a detached position from which to assemble a chaotic and inexplicable set of events so as to put the story and all it implies behind him.

Quentin Compson comes to us as an auditor who is forced to listen to Rosa Coldfield, to his father, to his roommate, but who struggles to resist a narrative pull that threatens to engulf him. In the novel's opening chapter, he defends against Rosa's insistent voice by retreating from its sound to a visual register in which he can try to maintain some sense of separation from the events being described. "Her voice would not cease it would just vanish," as Quentin watches a kind of freeze frame in which Sutpen "abrupt[s] ... the Sutpen's Hundred, the *Be Sutpen's Hundred* like the oldentime *Be Light*" (*AA*, 4). In this "soundless" vision even God's words have become objects, seen and not heard. Quentin visualizes the ghosts here, much as Hightower did, looking through his window at the imagined scene of his Grandfather's heroic charge, but with the opposite intent. Hightower is trying to return to the past in order to escape the present, while Quentin is trying to escape the past so as to enter the present. Quentin later tells Shreve, "I am older at twenty than a lot of people who have died" (*AA*, 301). He is, then, "two separate Quentins," one so absorbed by the stories of the past that he is virtually a ghost, the other struggling to live anew as a young man on the cusp of adulthood—always a key moment for Faulkner. The Quentin whose "very body [is] an empty hall echoing with sonorous defeated names" wants to shut his ears, but even when "listening would renege and hearing sense self-confound," he remains trapped in the past, "too young to deserve yet to be a ghost but nevertheless having to be one for all that" (*AA*, 4). Ironically, it is only when he engages in conversation, participates with Shreve in the "happy marriage of speaking and hearing," that Quentin gains the chance to free himself of the past (*AA*, 253). Remaining silent has only refueled the memories that make of him a "barracks, a commonwealth" rather than a single and autonomous person (*AA*, 7). Once the "two separate Quentins" converse and collude in telling the story, they not only uncover a bitter truth but enable a connection between past and present that recognizes rather than denies history.

Drawn forth and compelled to participate in the conversation, the reader resembles Shreve as well as Quentin. By the time Shreve appears on the scene in Chapter 6, it is important to realize, we already know the major events of Sutpen's life after his arrival in Jefferson. Indeed, by the end of Chapter 1 the whole story has virtually been put on record, although we don't know how to make sense of it. So when Shreve opens the discussion with his recital of what he's heard and his questions about what it means, the story is actually being repeated. We are in a position like Quentin's in Chapter 1 in the sense that we've heard it all already; what is said almost seems to strike "the resonant strings of remembering," as it did for Quentin (*AA*, 172). As a student of mine once remarked, reading *Absalom, Absalom!* is like life itself: once you're old enough to figure out what is going on, you're already partly responsible for it. As readers, once we have some grip on the main features of the story, we are partly responsible for it because we've participated in constructing it. Faulkner systematically implicates us in the storytelling from the outset.

How does this strategy work? We can observe it in miniature if we look at the scene in Chapter 2 when Sutpen arrives in Jefferson. A posse rides out to confront him, and he is described as follows: "He was riding the roan horse, in the frock coat and the beaver hat which they knew and with his legs wrapped in a piece of tarpaulin; he had a portmanteau on his pommel and he was carrying a small woven basket on his arm" (*AA*, 34). As Sutpen arrives at the Holston House, we are reminded again that he is still carrying "the portmanteau and the basket." What do they contain? We are not just invited to ask this question but teased with it. When Sutpen emerges from the hotel, we, along with the posse, learn the answer to one question, at least. "He wore a new hat now, and a new broadcloth coat, so they knew what the portmanteau had contained." So do we. But another question emerges when we are told "they even knew now what the basket had contained . . . though doubtless at the time it merely puzzled them more than ever" (*AA*, 35).

Now, irritatingly enough, the townspeople know something we don't—what was in the basket. Our suspense about this question is not relieved until the end of the next paragraph, when Sutpen finally reaches Mr. Coldfield's front steps, "carrying his newspaper cornucopia of flowers" (*AA*, 36). The sequencing of revelations here creates a serial suspense that keeps us going, through prose in which much else is said about Sutpen, creating a narrative pull that is fueled first by the need to find out what was in the two containers, and then by the need to understand what their contents signal as to Sutpen's intentions.

There are two kinds of gaps in knowledge put in counterpointed play here. There is the gap between what the townspeople know and what we know. Then there is the gap between knowing the "facts" and understanding what they mean; even when they see the flowers, the posse doesn't "get it," so preoccupied are they with their suspicions that Sutpen is a thief and murderer of some ill-defined sort. But having learned the contents of the portmanteau, we are likely already to understand what Sutpen is up to here—a marriage proposal for which he must dress up. If we make this inference, the revelation about the flowers serves as confirmation rather than revelation and also provides final relief from a long and highly ornate sentence. Here, in microcosm, is an essential feature of Faulkner's narrative strategy in the novel as a whole. On the one hand, he withholds information, leading us to read on in the hope of gaining it, and on the other hand, he possesses us of information that we don't know how to interpret or understand. Like the posse, for example, we may know something but fail to have the appropriate context for understanding it; indeed, we may be wholly misled by assumptions that turn out to be partial or groundless. No sooner is one question answered than another arises, and only in retrospect do certain pieces of information assume significance.

The structure of suspense building in this scene can serve as a synecdoche for the larger and far more complex narrative strategy on which the novel itself depends. The passage illustrates how Faulkner involves the reader at the most intimate and fundamental level in sharing the burden of storytelling. One may be ahead of or behind the game in anticipating the meaning of an event, but one is never allowed a secure vantage point from which it is possible to stand outside the picture and compose it except in the most provisional sense. For example, in Chapter 1 we wonder, as do other characters, why Rosa has summoned Quentin and what Rosa wants Quentin to do. Her suspicion that there is "something in that house" is not enunciated until the end of Chapter 5, and the first account of Quentin's journey with Rosa to Sutpen's Hundred only appears in Chapter 6 (*AA*, 140). The answer to our question, in other words, is delayed for four chapters. Even when we get that answer, it comes in the form of yet another question: if someone is "living ... hidden" in that house, who is it? For the answer to this second question, we must wait until Chapter 9, when Quentin finally recalls his encounter with Henry Sutpen. Again, we pick up enough information along the way to anticipate this outcome, that Bon is Henry's part-black half-brother, information that can only have come, in any definitive sense, from Henry. By the time the scene between Henry and Quentin is presented, we have a large investment in the crucial piece of information we have assumed Quentin received from him. We've heard the entire story of Sutpen's youth, his first marriage in Haiti, why he came to

Mississippi to start over, and why he compelled Henry to kill Bon. Thanks to Shreve's questions, we know what Quentin knows, and thanks to the brilliant retelling of the story enacted by Quentin and Shreve, we think we understand it. Both of the gaps have been crossed, but now a third one yawns before us, that between what we know and understand, on the one hand, and actual verification of the information presupposed by our knowledge and understanding. The conversation recorded between Quenin and Henry reveals only that it is Henry speaking. No confirmation of his relation to Bon is forthcoming.

> *And you are ------?*
> *Henry Sutpen.*
> *And you have been here -------?*
> *Four Years.*
> *And you came home -------?*
> *To die. Yes.*
> *To die?*
> *Yes. To die.*
> *And you have been here -------?*
> *Four Years.*
> *And you are -------?*
> *Henry Sutpen (AA, 298).*

This conversation not only denies us any confirming testimony but its self-mirroring form seems deliberately to rebuff our desire for verification.

This third gap has, of course, always been there. When Mr. Compson, for example, relates to Quentin what he knows of the Sutpen saga, he heavily sprinkles his account with disclaimers such as "doubtless," or "I suppose." He is fully aware that even the letter he shows Quentin cannot provide hard evidence for his account. It has neither a specified addressee nor a signature, and only the story of Judith's giving it to Quentin's grandmother as testimony to its authenticity. Quentin and Shreve freely imagine much of the tale they tell, including making up characters like the lawyer who works for Eulalia Bon, since they need him to explain Bon's otherwise inexplicable appearance in Mississippi. If we focus primarily on this third gap, as critics so often have, it is easy to regard the novel as essentially a self-reflexive modernist exercise, demonstrating how all meaning is finally fictional. But as *Light in August* should serve to remind us, just because people make things up doesn't keep those things from having real consequences. If fictions can regress into collective myths that make for "good believing" among racists, fiction making can also provoke imaginative engagements with the socially given, cutting through layers of ideologies to reveal their betrayal of human possibility. As a southerner, Faulkner was particularly well situated to understand how fictions could construct and misconstruct history in the interests of a particular viewpoint, and he was certainly fully in touch with the modernist realization that we live within frameworks constructed and reconstructed with words. But in *Absalom, Absalom!* he was concerned with more than demonstrating the South's delusions, and more than rehearsing the modernist's sometimes complacently ironic stance, although Rosa and Mr. Compson, respectively, accomplish these ends. He was devoted to developing a narrative strategy that compels us to participate in telling the story in order to make us realize, and take responsibility for, the fact that we live inside of history, not behind some window looking out at it, like Hightower. Much as Hightower is drawn forth into life, however briefly, by Byron Bunch's efforts, the reader is drawn forth into history understood as the "stream of event," a stream that includes language, "that meagre and fragile thread...by which the little surface corners and edges of men's secret and solitary lives may be joined for an instant now and then" (*AA*, 202). In the course of their intense imagining, Quentin and Shreve are thus "joined," if only briefly, in the "happy marriage of speaking and hearing" (*AA*, 253). Further, when they are "joined" by Henry and Charles, becoming Quentin/Henry and Shreve/Bon, the line dividing them from the story they are telling dissolves, merging the narrators they are with the characters they are imagining within one "stream of event" (*AA*, 127).

What compelled this radical formal invention, the most ambitious and complex of Faulkner's career, was the figure of Thomas Sutpen, a man whose history and fate offered the prospect not only of continuing the effort begun in *Light in August* to address the devastating impact of racial division on his society, but also of deepening the focus so as to address the interaction of race, class, and gender, and broadening his canvas so as to encompass America. At the height of his powers as a writer, Faulkner could now take full advantage of the critical distance he had established on the South. Having invented his county, he was now able to situate it in relation to America and its past.

Thomas Sutpen's story, once it is fully told, is actually several stories in one. One of these is the story of the southern slaveholding planter, emblem of the South itself, brought down by its own hubris and inhumanity. Another is the story of the fall of the house of Agamemnon, killed in part because he has sacrificed his own daughter in the interest of his design for warmaking. Another is the story of King David, retold with an emphasis on the father's loss of his son Absalom who has slept with his sister. Another is the story of the boy Sutpen, who suffers such an affront to his identity as white, male, and equal that he sets out to emulate precisely the man who has insulted him, thereby stepping into the central role in the American Dream. Unlike Joe Christmas, the character of Thomas Sutpen refers us to many symbolic frameworks, not just one. It is therefore impossible to account for his career from any single perspective, but it is just as impossible to do justice to all of the perspectives the novel and its storytellers bring to bear. I want, then, to suggest only a few of the many ways of understanding Sutpen.

To begin with, if we are to understand Sutpen at all, we must appreciate his "innocence," as Grandfather Compson calls it. He is the bearer of tragic innocence, of course. As Faulkner said, "The Greeks destroyed him, the old Greek concept of tragedy" (*University,* 35). That is, like Oedipus, Sutpen is innocent in the sense of being ignorant; he does not and cannot know that his every step takes him closer to his fated destiny. Each effort he makes to achieve his design leads to its undoing. But Faulkner builds on the Greek concept of tragic innocence, making of Sutpen's innocence a crucial register of the social structures he is forced to combat. Sutpen never loses his innocence, but his life purpose is defined at the moment he discovers it.

Having "fallen" into the domain of large plantations in Tidewater, Virginia, with his family, Sutpen confronts a world that bears no resemblance to his Appalachian birthplace. Where he has grown up, "the land belonged to anybody and everybody and so the man who would go to the trouble and work to fence off a piece of it and say 'This is mine' was crazy" (*AA,* 179). Only such a crazy man would try to take and keep more than he needs. If a man possesses something of value, like a fine rifle, it would never occur to him to think or say "*because I own this rifle, my arms and legs and blood and bones are superior to yours* except as the victorious outcome of a fight with rifles" (*AA,* 185). Like Locke's vision of the state of nature, the primitive culture from which Sutpen comes is radically simple. If some people have more than others, it is only because they are "lucky." No one seeks to own more than he and his family need, and no one looks down on anyone else except the Indians, "and you only looked down at them over your rifle sights" (*AA,* 179). The Tidewater, on the other hand, is "a country all divided and fixed and neat with a people living on it all divided and fixed and neat because of what color their skins happened to be and what they happened to own" (*AA,* 179). In this world there is a difference "not only between white men and black ones," but also "between white men and white men not to be measured by lifting anvils or gouging eyes or how much whiskey you could drink then get up and walk out of the room" (*AA,* 183).

The young Thomas Sutpen regards this new world with curiosity and awe, but not envy. It is not until he is sent up to the big white house with a message from his father and turned away from the front door by the black butler that he confronts the fact that he has no place in it. Having observed the planter in his scuppernong arbor, Sutpen looks forward to seeing the inside of the house, "never for one moment thinking but what the man would be pleased to show him" (*AA*, 185–186). Having come in the "good faith of business, which he had believed all men accepted," Sutpen is suddenly faced with what he and his family actually are in the eyes of the planter: "cattle, creatures heavy and without grace, brutely evacuated into a world without hope or purpose for them" (*AA*, 190). When he returns home, this is precisely how he sees his sister, "broad in the beam as a cow, the very labor she was doing brutish and stupidly out of all proportion to its reward" (*AA*, 191). But the worst is yet to come. His father doesn't even bother to ask whether he has delivered the message. Nor, apparently, has the planter sent anyone down to find out why his father had failed to do the work for which the message was, Sutpen surmises, probably an excuse. "He never even gave me a chance to say it and Pap never asked me if I told him or not and so he cant even know that Pap sent him any message and so whether he got it or not can't even matter, not even to Pap." It is at this moment that the "explosion" happens, "a bright glare that vanished and left nothing, no ashes or refuse, just a limitless flat plain with the severe shape of his intact innocence rising from it like a monument" (*AA*, 192). Sutpen at once faces and violently repudiates his impotence, an impotence whose discovery immediately produces the phallic monument in which it is at once enshrined and disavowed.

It is now his "innocence instructing him," explaining that to "combat them" he will need to acquire what they have; "you got to have land and niggers and a fine house to combat them with." Seeking an adequate form for revenge, the voice of his innocence becomes his conscience, the arbiter and guide who dictate what he must do if he is to "combat them" (*AA*, 192).

Thus is the design born, in the mind of a boy of fourteen or so, roughly, the age of Huckleberry Finn. As he later tells Grandfather Compson, "I had a design. To accomplish it I should require money, a house, a plantation, slaves, a family—incidentally, of course, a wife" (*AA*, 212). By family, of course, he means not just children, but a son, the bearer of his name into the future.

We can now make a few observations about Sutpen's innocence. For one thing, it consists in his retention of the belief in the rule of physical force, the rule he learned as a child on the frontier. Some men may be stronger than others, or luckier, say, but their power over other men can only be proven as a result of combat. Thus Sutpen will ritually stage wrestling matches with his slaves, as if needing to confirm his superiority to them through actual, physical fights. He first seizes power in Haiti, of course, by violently putting down a slave rebellion. Sutpen's physical courage wins him a citation for valor from Lee himself; even Rosa acknowledges that he was brave. As he tells General Compson, "He believed that all necessary was courage and shrewdness and the one he knew he had and the other he believed he could learn if it were to be taught" (*AA*, 197). Sutpen's "shrewdness," however effective in enabling him to acquire land and wealth when he comes to Jefferson, is marked by a certain simplicity. As he tells his story in Chapter 7, Grandfather Compson listens in amazement to his meticulous justification for abandoning his first wife and their child, hearing "that innocence again, that innocence which believed that the ingredients of morality were like the ingredients of pie or cake and once you had measured them and balanced them and mixed them and put them into the oven it was all finished and nothing but pie or cake could come out" (*AA*, 211–212). (Even cooking requires more imagination than this, as the case of Cora Tull illustrates.) Because he has been so careful in following the recipe dictated by his design, its failure must, he believes, be due to some "mistake" he has made, a "mistake which he could not discover himself and which he came to grandfather," Quentin says, "not to excuse but just to review the facts for an impartial . . . mind to examine and find and point out to him" (*AA*, 215). If he can identify the mistake, Sutpen believes, he can "still combat" it (*AA*, 215). General Compson wails at him and at the "purblind innocence" that persuades him that he could do such violence to his wife and child without fear of retribution (*AA*, 213).

In both its alignment with the frontier rule of violence and its faith in the kind of legalistic reasoning that enables him to escape his contract with his first father-in-law due to the alleged deceit of which he was a victim, Sutpen's innocence is deeply rooted in American history, from the violent expulsion of the Indians through the "good faith of business" required to build a capitalist economy. But more fundamentally American is Sutpen's quest to prove, as the Declaration of Independence puts it, that "all men are created equal," or, as Faulkner said in describing Sutpen to the students at Virginia, "that man, if he is man, cannot be inferior to another man through artificial standards or circumstances" (*University*, 35). In Sutpen's terms, some people are "spawned rich . . . and some not," but that is a matter of "luck," not superiority. His design is aimed at proving that any boy, whatever "nameless stranger," "would never again need to stand on the outside of a white door and knock at it," because future generations would have "been riven forever free from brutehood" by Sutpen's successful combat in their name (*AA*, 210).

Yet clearly, in his effort to vindicate the principle of social equality, Sutpen reconstitutes the very class structure he set out to oppose. His design dictates that in order to prove that any little boy can live in the big white house, he must acquire the house itself and all that goes with it, and in so doing, he rises above and finally refuses recognition to the man who mirrors Sutpen's own origins—Wash Jones. In denying Jones the social recognition he finally demands, Sutpen brings his own life to a violent end, and provokes Jones himself to suicide and the massacre of his offspring. Jones, who has accepted being denied entrance even to Sutpen's back door, now faces the fact that Sutpen himself had once faced the planter's front door, that he is precisely the insignificant creature for which Sutpen's slaves have always taken him. "Better if his kind and mine too had never drawn the breath of life on this earth," he thinks, than to live without the respect owed by free men to one another (*AA*, 233).

The question here, as with every other outcome of Sutpen's design, is how he can be so blind in the face of the responses his actions are likely to provoke. The answer lies in that innocence, long embedded in the design out of which it first emerges. As we have noticed, the boy Sutpen has no way of understanding why the planter behaves as he does, or why the butler behaves as he does, and he never understands it. Instead, he sets out to emulate what he sees, to mimic the man who "spent most of the afternoon ... in a barrel stave hammock between two trees, with his shoes off and a nigger ... who did nothing else but fan him and bring him drinks" (*AA*, 184). In what amounts to a lifelong performance, he sets out to acquire what the owner has acquired, the symbols of his superiority. His eye is forever after on the combat he thereby sees himself engaged in, to prove that he is the planter's equal. But the design itself simply mirrors the Tidewater planter's achieved social eminence, thereby *reflecting* the society over which the planter presides, but *never comprehending* the conflicts and contradictions inherent in that society. Sutpen's career in pursuit of his design, then, can serve to expose these contradictions to us for the same reason they remain utterly obscure to Sutpen himself; he has no capacity to see them because they are frozen within the image he sets out to emulate. Thus, his design is aimed at proving that all men are worthy of recognition as free and equal, but it works out to reveal and indeed to reconfirm that they are not. By the same token, the design compels Sutpen to found a dynasty, but it also compels him to repudiate his own son. Because the contradictions inhere in the design itself, Sutpen cannot see them and searches always for the "mistake" he has made in following the recipe. The peculiar power of such a character lies in its capacity to confront American society with its own image, specifically to expose two social contradictions: (1) the one between the claim to social equality and the denial in practice of that claim because of both race and class, and (2) the one between the claims of paternalism to foster the welfare of the family and the actual drive of patriarchy to pass on the father's name.

The novel is, of course, focused on the South, but it is a South that is rooted in the larger history of America. Certainly, Faulkner wanted to explode what he called the "makebelieve region of swords and magnolias and mockingbirds" (*S&F*, 229), but in this novel he wanted to do more than that. Just as his narrative strategy enabled him to reveal the romantic compulsions and guilt-ridden denials that fed the "makebelieve" visions of the Old South, his construction of Sutpen enabled him to represent the South as emerging from within American history, and providing a particularly salient vantage point from which to see its contradictions. Thus, Sutpen's character radically undermines the nostalgic picture of the southern white planter whose paternalistic ideology ostensibly redeemed him from the sin of slave owning, but it does so by revealing that the would-be aristocratic planter figure was actually only a successful capitalist entrepreneur. Claiming that he was a benevolent father figure, the southern planter both before and after the civil war took pride in representing a clear moral alternative to the "wage-slavery" he saw in the North. In fact, he was daily extracting forced labor from his slaves, but he claimed to think of them as his children, the irony being, of course, that they often were his children, as Sutpen's case serves to emphasize. It is significant as well that Sutpen's primitive accumulation of capital takes place in Haiti, pointing to the larger scope of the economic forces that generated the development of slave labor in the Americas. Another indication of the scope of Faulkner's "design" is the choice of a Canadian, Shreve McCannon, rather than a northerner, as Quentin's interlocutor. So while Sutpen's design mirrors the world of the southern planter before the civil war, that world itself is as much American as it is southern. If we focus in particular on Sutpen's origins in—as Shreve insists that Quentin acknowledge—what was not even yet West Virginia, his background aligns him with the American frontier, as well as with a state that did not secede from the union.

As we have seen in the case of Wash Jones, Sutpen's design dictates that he deny recognition to the poor white, whose social origins he shares. But this is not the most harrowing of the contradictions exposed by Sutpen's campaign to prove that all men are created equal. The most devastating contradiction that emerges is between American freedom and American slavery. As Edmund Morgan long ago demonstrated, it was the labor of slaves that produced the tobacco on which "the position of the United States depended not only in 1776 but during the span of a long lifetime thereafter."[3] "King Tobacco Diplomacy" was to be followed by King Cotton, whose economic significance Faulkner was to underscore in *Go Down, Moses,* describing cotton as "cable-strong to bind for life them who made the cotton to the land their sweat fell on."[4] Not only economically but also politically, white freedom was forged by the denial of black freedom, a fact whose social consequences are registered in Wash Jones's tenuous hold on his social identity as a free man. The racial difference "between white men and black men" enables the denial of the class difference between white men and white men, but only up to a certain point. When Sutpen repudiates responsibility for Milly, Jones's grand daughter, it is because she has borne a girl, not a boy. "Well, Milly," Sutpen says, "too bad you're not a mare too. Then I could give you a decent stall in the stable," like the one in which his mare, Penelope, has just borne a "damned fine colt" (*AA*, 229). Although he hardly seems suited to the role, Wash Jones acts out the role of a father, killing Sutpen in order to avenge the insult to his newborn great-granddaughter. When Sutpen repudiates Charles Bon because (he thinks) he is black, not white, Sutpen is also, ironically enough, acting in the name of fatherhood.

Neither a girl nor a black can bear the name of the father, and therefore neither can be "adjunctive" to Sutpen's design.

The second contradiction exposed by Sutpen's design, then, concerns race and gender, and emerges as the result of the design's replication of a dynastic patriarchy. A student at Virginia made so bold as to ask Faulkner whether Sutpen ever acknowledged Clytie as his daughter. Faulkner patiently replied that "it would not have mattered" whether he did so, since she was "female," and Sutpen would "have to have a male descendant" if he was going to create a "dukedom" (*University*, 272). Sutpen, Faulkner elsewhere noted, wanted to "establish a dynasty," to "make himself a king and raise a line of princes" (*University*, 98). The novel makes clear that the father, to be a father, must pass on the name of the father to a son, who in turn can pass it on to "the fine grandsons and great-grandsons springing as far as eye could reach" (*AA*, 218). As Grandfather Compson says, at the time Sutpen abandoned Charles and his mother Eulalia, he "would not permit the child, since it was a boy, to bear either his name or that of its maternal grandfather," and yet neither would he "do the customary and provide a quick husband for the discarded woman and so give his son an authentic name" (*AA*, 214). Charles is barred not only from bearing Sutpen's name but from bearing any paternal name because he is the bearer of so-called black blood. Why should this be so important? The matrilineal rule of slavery dictates that the child must follow the "condition" of the mother. Accordingly, the black mother, in becoming a mother, erases, blots out, the name of the father, thereby reducing all of her sons to the status of "boys," that is, men legally incapable of becoming fathers. As Shreve phrases it, as the black son of a white father,

Charles Bon inevitably "inherited what he was from his mother and only what he could never have been from his father" (*AA*, 174). The racial discourse of "blood" that a black son introduces into the dynastic line Sutpen aims to found leads to a serial catastrophe that not only dooms Sutpen's design, but also lays bare the social structure of patriarchy.

The roles to which women are assigned in the novel testify to the subordination dictated by patriarchal rule. As Deborah Clarke has shown, Sutpen's infamous "proposal" to Rosa in effect blurts out what woman's primary function under patriarchy actually is, "to become a womb to bring forth male children."[5] By rejecting Sutpen, Rosa turns down the one escape she is offered from being an aging spinster. Yet her exclusion from the role of wife and mother has made her into a formidable agent of revenge, as she speaks for, and acts on behalf of, Ellen Coldfield as well as Eulalia Bon, and even Milly Jones—the mothers who failed to meet Sutpen's genealogical demands. Further, her exclusion from any sexual experience turns her into "all polymath love's androgynous advocate" in Chapter 5, where she gives voice to a passion that her culture denies to women, unless they occupy the role of octoroon mistress (*AA*, 117). Rosa may be dismissed as deranged, but she is after all "a character cold, implacable, and even ruthless," much like Sutpen himself (*AA*, 6).

A full picture of the novel's intricate treatment of both gender and race relations would take a chapter to itself, at the least. What seems to me crucial in understanding Faulkner's approach to these issues is the plight of Charles Bon and Henry Sutpen, as their dilemma illustrates the critical feature of fatherhood as experienced from the son's perspective—the need for recognition. Over and against the abstract and instru-mental version of patriarchy embedded in Sutpen's design, there is the all too personal and compelling experience of the sons and brothers trapped in combat with each other as a result of Sutpen's refusal to recognize Bon as his son. From the son's standpoint as represented by Bon, the passing on of the father's name is merely a legal marker for what actually matters—that his father recognize him. As Quentin and Shreve imagine him, Bon is perfectly willing to withdraw and disappear if Sutpen will only give him a sign of recognition. When he challenges Henry to try and stop him from marrying Judith, Charles is insisting, even unto death, that he be recognized. In a sense, when Henry kills him, Bon is finally recognized, yet he is recognized not as Sutpen's son but as "the nigger who's going to sleep with [Henry's] sister" (*AA*, 286). In forcing the issue, Bon is wreak-ing his own revenge for his father's refusal to recognize him, making Henry into a murderer and leaving Judith a "widow" before she can become a "bride."

Recognition is a central issue in this novel. Indeed, it is fair to say that the novel as a whole is organized around a series of scenes in which recognition is demanded and denied: Sutpen turned away from the big white house by the black butler; Wash Jones turned away from the back door by the black Clytie; Rosa confronted by Clytie at the foot of the stairs; Quentin paralyzed at the memory of passing the door into Henry's room; Henry stopping Bon at the front gate to their father's house. Not surprisingly, then, thresholds, doors and gates, serve repeatedly as the site of violent and sometimes lethal confrontation. Henry, for example, waits until they reach the gatepost of Sutpen's Hundred before turning on Bon. Then when Henry comes to the door alone, the encounter between brother and sister is described as a physical struggle: "speaking to one another in short brief staccato sentences like slaps, as if they stood breast to breast striking one another in turn, neither making any attempt to guard against the blows: Now you cant marry him. Why cant I marry him? Because he's dead. Dead? Yes, I killed him" (*AA*, 139–140). Recognition, it seems, cannot take place except through some form of violent physical contact, as the crucial scene between Rosa and Clytie indicates.

When Rosa arrives at Sutpen's Hundred in response to Wash Jones's announcement that Henry has shot Bon, she enters the front hall calling for Judith. But instead she is met by Clytie, a "furious yet absolutely rocklike and immobile antagonism" who says to her "Don't you go up there, Rosa" (*AA*, 110–111). Rosa is shocked at Clytie's use of her Christian name, a familiarity that constitutes a kind of insult between black slave and white lady. But even as she reacts aloud with the proper indignation— "Rosa? . . . To me? To my face?" (*AA*, 111)—Rosa actually sees past this offense. It is no excuse that Clytie had called her Rosa as a child, just as she had called Judith and Henry by their first names and still does. In fact it is because Clytie recognizes her as a force to be contended with, a person to be opposed, that Rosa realizes that "she did me more grace and respect than anyone else I knew," since "from the instant I had entered that door, to her of all who knew me I was no child." While acting out the appropriate racist response, Rosa experiences a kind of recognition shockingly new to her, someone whom "everyone else" still sees, at nineteen, "as a child." Then, in the second stage of the traumatic encounter, Clytie puts out her hand to stop Rosa, who is "stop[ped] dead" by "that black arresting and untimorous hand on my white woman's flesh" (*AA*, 111) Again, Rosa responds aloud according to code: "Take your hand off me, nigger!" But silently she registers a connection with Clytie and ends up silently calling Clytie "sister," acknowledging that she and Clytie are "twinsistered to the fell darkness which had produced her" (*AA*, 112). When Judith calls Clytie off, the moment closes and Rosa returns to her unrecognized status as child; Judith won't even let her into the room where Bon's body lies. But the scene reveals the deep human need for connection that drives the demand for recognition itself.

In *Absalom, Absalom!*, recognition is restricted (or legitimized) by class, race, and gender, generating a cultural system that denies the physical connections on which any human community depends. Sutpen's design reifies that system, and its colossal failure exposes the fault lines in the social structure it tries to replicate. But the need for connection that Sutpen's design ignores is abundantly addressed in the novel's narrative form, where an ongoing conversation serves not only to connect the people talking, but to connect them with people long dead. In this respect, Judith's gesture in passing on Bon's letter to Mrs. Compson is at least as significant as its contents: "you are born at the same time with a lot of other people, . . . all trying to make a rug on the same loom only each one wants to weave his own pattern into the rug." Finally, you die, and someone puts up a tombstone with "scratches on it," and so "it doesn't matter" after all. But then, she says, "maybe if you could go to someone, the stranger the better, and give them something—a scrap of paper—something, anything, . . . it would be something just because it would have happened, be remembered even if only from passing from one hand to another, one mind to another"

(*AA*, 100–101). Judith responds, we could put it, to impotence—the failure to make an impression which led her father to conceive his design, as well as to bring home two blocks of marble to mark his and his wife's grave—with the simple physical act of passing something on to someone. Judith's contrast with her father is further emphasized by the fact that the letter itself embodies the same principle as the act of passing it on; it is a message passed on from "one mind to another" and in particular, passed from brother to sister, reconnecting the blood relation Sutpen had denied, many years after he himself had failed to pass on a message. Bon's letter, as well as Judith's act, manifest physically the principle of connection at work in all the novel's conversations. All the speaking and hearing, dominated though it may be by a single narrative voice, represents an ongoing social act of the imagination. Although it cannot found a dynasty, it can create a community of sorts.

Faulkner published two more novels after *Absalom, Absalom!* that were to join it as among his finest: *The Hamlet* (1940) and *Go Down, Moses* (1942). Both of these novels were written in roughly the same fashion as was *The Unvanquished*, by revising and stitching together short stories, most of which Faulkner had already composed. Because it is thematically tied so closely to *Absalom, Absalom!*, I want to address *Go Down Moses* first. *The Hamlet* would become the first, and indisputably the best, of the Snopes Trilogy, to be completed in the 1950s with *The Town* and *The Mansion*. Since "Snopes," as Faulkner sometimes called the trilogy itself, stems from works written as early as the 1920s and represents a fundamentally distinct, and comic, thread in Faulkner's career, I shall return to it in the next chapter.

Here, before turning to *Go Down, Moses,* it seems appropriate to note that Faulkner's imagination was by no means limited to Yoknapatawpha. Like his long sentences, the "little postage stamp of native soil" that Faulkner invented is often taken to define the "Faulknerian" for us. But Faulkner wrote short sentences too, perhaps most memorably "My mother is a fish." And he wrote stories and novels, not to mention screenplays, that were not set in Yoknapatawpha. Two of these, *Pylon* (1935) and *The Wild Palms* (1939), whose working title, *If I Forget Thee, O Jerusalem,* has been restored by its editor Noel Polk, were written during the years between *Absalom, Absalom!* and both *The Hamlet* and *Go Down Moses,* and have sometimes been underestimated at least in part because they don't fit into the Yoknapatawpha scheme of things. Yet both are important novels whose brilliance would show up more clearly were they not chronologically flanked by the clear genius of the three major novels written during the same period.

Pylon is the less ambitious of the two, written at forced draft in the last two months of 1934 when Faulkner was stumped as to how to proceed with *Absalom, Absalom!,* which he had begun in February. Based on his recent experience with the barnstorming fliers he had met when taking flying lessons (at last), *Pylon* focuses on a strangely composed family—Roger Shumann and his wife Laverne, Jiggs the mechanic, a parachute jumper named Holmes who travels and performs with them, and Laverne's son Jack, whose father may be Shumann or may be Holmes. "Who's your old man today, kid?" Jiggs asks Jack repeatedly, knowing the question will immediately provoke the boy's fighting stance.[6] The issue of fatherhood, in short, never entirely disappears from Faulkner's mind, here underscoring the absence of a traditional father figure. Set in "New Valois," a not even disguised version of New Orleans, the novel portrays the lives of modern nomads, adventurers who have chosen to fly, both literally and figuratively, rather than to settle anywhere. Unbound to any conventional homes or commitments, they travel the countryside competing in airplane shows and putting on demonstrations. Virtually an antithesis to the well known "Faulknerian" scene of gothic sins and visceral horrors, *Pylon* takes on the urban and the modern, portraying it as both soulless and frantically heroic. The barnstormers' world is opened to view through the eyes of the nameless "Reporter," who wants to write them up for the newspaper and becomes enthralled both by Laverne and by the world she and her men inhabit, if that term can be used. As if charged by the Mardi Gras setting, the prose style assumes a manic, sometimes outlandish, aspect: "Overhead, beyond the palmtufts, the overcast sky reflected that interdict and lightglared canyon now adrift with serpentine and confetti, through which the floats, bearing grimacing and antic mimes dwarfed chalkwhite and forlorn and contemplated by static curbmass of amazed confettifaces, passed as though through steady rain" (*P*, 53). Ernest Hemingway, although stylistically Faulkner's opposite, apparently liked the novel, but he did not represent the majority view of the critics.

More successful, both critically and commercially was *The Wild Palms*, which appeared in the same month, January 1939, that Faulkner's picture graced the cover of *Time* magazine. Maurice Coindreau had begun translating Faulkner's fiction into French, and the National Institute of Arts and Letters had invited Faulkner to become a member. Critics responded more favorably to "Old Man," the half of the novel that dealt with a convict caught up in the great flood of 1927, than to the other half entitled "The Wild Palms," which dealt with a love affair between a young medical student and a married woman with two children. Most were puzzled at the question of how to relate the one to the other. The question has never been fully answered. What we do know is that Faulkner wrote them as they were finally published, moving from one story to the other. The convict's story, later anthologized on its own, provides a powerful account of a flood and what it feels like to find oneself in the middle of one. The constitutive irony of the story is that the convict, who ends up having to save a pregnant woman, bring her child into the world, and support her by killing alligators for a while, is ready and eager to return to the entirely masculine safety of the prison, once he is "rescued." The story of Charlotte Rittenmeyer and Harry Wilbourne directly coun- terpoints that of the "tall convict" by tracing an intense sexual intimacy from its beginning through the death of Charlotte, thanks to a botched abortion performed, unwillingly, by Harry. Like the convict, Harry is in prison at the story's end, but unlike the convict, whose final line is "Women. Shit," Harry rejects suicide in order to keep alive his memory of Charlotte: "Between grief and nothing, I'll take grief," he says.[7]

The Wild Palms sold better than any previous novel of Faulkner's, including *Sanctuary,* more than a thousand copies a week by March. The critics remained puzzled, but recognized the power of his writing even if they couldn't fathom the point of its complexity. The *Time* article both acknowledged and forwarded a reputation that was by now too noteworthy to ignore. *The Wild Palms* was Faulkner's eleventh novel, and in both Europe and South America, he was being read in translation by sophisticated and attentive critics and writers. Meanwhile, in Oxford he had acquired thirty-five acres of land adjacent to Rowan Oak. Using the proceeds from the sale of the screen rights to *The Unvanquished*, he had also bought what he named "Greenfield Farm" outside town and set his brother up as its manager. Although Johncy wanted to raise cattle, as their father would certainly have advised, Faulkner insisted that they raise mules—his favorite animal. He had suffered deep pain over the recent loss of Meta Carpenter to another man, pain to which "The Wild Palms" story was in many ways a response. (Meta would come back into his life from time to time, but their affair was over.) Despite this anguish, he was in a sense at the peak of his powers. He immediately began putting together and revising the stories that he would later compose into the novel *The Hamlet*, upon whose publication he would immediately begin weaving together *Go Down, Moses* in the same fashion. But in both cases, he was working against a strong headwind that would hit him squarely by July 1942, when he returned to Hollywood on a seven-year contract with Warner Brothers. For most of the 1940s, Faulkner would struggle against the demands of Hollywood in order to maintain his devotion to meeting the demands of his own imagination.

Go Down, Moses in some ways seems to follow quite logically the strategies of *Absalom,Absalom!* In both novels, the reader is called on to make vital connections in order to find the sense of the narrative. One could even argue that there is a kind of surrogate reader in each novel. Ike McCaslin is a reader in part four of "The Bear," poring over ledgers to find the truth, much as Quentin is represented as sitting at a table with "his hands lying on either side of the open textbook on which the letter rested" (*AA*, 176). Or perhaps Shreve is the more apt surrogate for the reader, as he brings to the conversation an outsider's questions and scrutiny. But no sooner do we see these possible analogies than they reveal themselves as limited. If the basic vehicle of narration in *Absalom, Absalom!* is conversation, in *Go Down, Moses* the story unfolds across several registers, from the incantatory voice that describes and reiterates Ike's initiation into the "big woods," to the third-person narrator who aligns our perspective with that of Lucas in "The Fire and the Hearth," or with Gavin Stevens's in "Go Down, Moses." There are indeed conversations here, but they do not link to each other in the fashion of *Absalom, Absalom!* Ike and his cousin Cass talk back and forth but their speech enacts a developing discord rather than "the happy marriage of speaking and hearing" momentarily celebrated by Quentin and Shreve in Chapter 8 (*AA*, 253). If Charles Bon's letter embodies what he calls an "apt commentary on the times and augur of the future," composed as it is of the French watermarked stationery of the Old South and the stove polish of the New North, the ledger Ike scrutinizes reaches well beyond such whimsical and ironic prophecy (*AA*, 102). The ledger is a "chronicle which was a whole land in miniature, which multiplied and compounded was the entire South," tracing as it does the path of "cotton—the two threads frail as truth and impalpable as equators yet cable-strong to bind for life them who made the cotton to the land their sweat fell on" (*GDM*, 281). What in *Absalom, Absalom!* was the "meager and fragile thread" of language here becomes the "cable-strong" thread of cotton production—the "slow trickle of molasses and meal and meat" outward from the commissary which returns "each fall as cotton" (*GDM*, 281).

Struggling to encompass not just the history, but the prehistory of slavery, *Go Down, Moses* is a more ambitious and more troubled work than *Absalom, Absalom!*

Consider the difference between Thomas Sutpen and Lucius Quintus Carothers McCaslin. To Rosa, Quentin, and Mr. Compson at least, Thomas Sutpen seems an anomaly. That is, his behavior is peculiar, not to the South, like its "peculiar institution," but peculiar precisely because it does not conform to the image they share of the patriarchal southern planter. What makes Sutpen not just peculiar but unintelligible, in General Compson's view, is his refusal to "do the customary" by finding a suitable husband for the wife he has rejected, thereby providing a name for the son he has disowned (*AA*, 214). By contrast, in *Go Down, Moses*, Faulkner begins with an all-too-typical southern planter, L.Q.C. McCaslin. This white, male patriarch fully embodies the Southern Planter, at least a Mississippi version of him. Born in Carolina before the American revolution, McCaslin arrives in the backcountry of Mississippi two generations earlier than Sutpen, with an abundance of slaves and the title to a large plantation he has bought from the Natives. Like Sutpen, he goes to New Orleans—perpetual source of exotic mulatto women, apparently—but not to investigate a black son's identity. Rather, he goes there to purchase a woman, Eunice, whom he clearly already knows. When she bears his child, Lucius provides Eunice with a husband, Thucydus, so as to cover his miscegenous activities in the conventional way. It is only when he sleeps with his own daughter that Lucius McCaslin seems to have seen himself as perhaps violating some code or other. Accordingly, he leaves $1,000.00 in his will to Tomasina's child, Tomy's Turl, a sum that Buck and Buddy triple in their allotment to Tomy's Turl's three living children. So both incest and miscegenation—the twin horrors that Henry Sutpen struggles for four years to ward off—have not only actually occurred, but the facts are known to Lucius's sons, Buck and Buddy, who both feel the need to compensate somehow for their father's sins. In this novel, it is not a set of facts unveiled but still warded off, but the unremitting guilt to which such facts lead that Ike confronts when he reads and finally deciphers the ledgers. The fact of miscegenation is apparently disputed by no one, least of all L.Q.C. McCaslin. The fact of incest is inferred from Eunice's suicide, which Buck and Buddy may dispute, but which more than confirms their suspicion that their father impregnated his own daughter, their half-sister. As for Ike, the only dispute he has is with his cousin Cass, who must be told about Ike's chosen method for atoning for the McCaslin family's treatment of its black members. Consequently, *Go Down, Moses* is driven less by suspense than by the need to confront and atone for the sins of the past, sins that are still being committed in the present.

Go Down, Moses (1942) is made up of seven short stories, some revised from earlier versions, which join each other in pursuit of a solution to the impasse created by slavery, both its history and its heritage. Scene and vehicle of both is the genealogy of a family surnamed McCaslin, in which there are three sets of descendants. The first of these is the white patriarchal line that begins with Lucius Quintus Carothers McCaslin (1772–1837) whose son Theophilus, known as Uncle Buck, marries Sophonsiba Beauchamp; from this union one son is born, Isaac McCaslin (b. 1867), who marks the end of this line of descent, as he has no children. The second line, descending by the "distaff" or female side of the family stems from the patriarch McCaslin's daughter who marries one Isaac Edmonds. From this line descends Carothers McCaslin Edmonds (b. 1850), called Cass, who has a son named Zack Edmonds (b. 1873), who in turn has a son named Roth Edmunds (b. 1898). The third line descends from the patriarch, but through unions with slave women. Old Carothers sleeps with a slave named Eunice, bringing forth a daughter, Tomasina. Then he sleeps with that daughter Tomasina, to bring forth a boy named Terrel, called "Tomey's Turl." The slave line of descent bears eventually the name Beauchamp because Terrel marries Tennie Beauchamp, as a result of the events recorded in the opening story, "Was." Among Terrel and Tennie's many children is Lucas Beachamp (b. 1874), who marries Molly Worsham, and the story of this old couple dominates "The Fire and the Hearth."

So there are three branches to this family, but only two that have a potential genealogical future: the white Edmonds, descended from the female side of McCaslin, and the black Beauchamps, descended from the male side of McCaslin, (but notably bearing the name of the mother, Tennie Beauchamp). Ike McCaslin repudiates his inheritance, leaving it to his Edmonds cousins, and adopts an alternative paternity by bonding with Sam Fathers and dedicating himself to the masculine world of the hunt and the wilderness. Sam himself has a mixed heritage, as is indicated by his full name, Sam Had-Two-Fathers. Sam's biological father was an Indian chief, Ikkemotubbe, but his mother was a black slave. He has two fathers because Ikkemotubbe sold him and his parents to L.G.C. McCaslin. Like Ike, Sam has no children, finding in the woods and the rituals of the hunt a stronger source for identity and value than any available in the town or on a farm.

It is useful to lay out these family lines because the novel itself exhibits no visible sense of responsibility for tracing them. On the contrary, it seems dedicated to mixing them up. Consider the opening sentence of "Was."

> Isaac McCaslin, 'Uncle Ike', past seventy and nearer eighty than he ever corroborated any more, a widower now and uncle to half a county and father to no one
>
>   this was not something participated in or even seen by himself, but by his elder cousin, McCaslin Edmonds, grandson of Isaac's father's sister and so descended by the distaff, yet notwithstanding the inheritor, and in his time the bequestor, of that which some had thought then and some still thought should have been Isaac's, since his was the name in which the title to the land had first been granted from the Indian patent and which some of the descendants of his father's slaves still bore in the land. But Isaac was not one of these (*GDM*, 3)

Although broken into paragraphs, the sentence itself persists without punctuation until the following page and the close of this, section one of the story:

> Not something he had participated in or even remembered except from the hearing, the listening, come to him through and from his cousin McCaslin born in 1850 and sixteen years his senior and hence, his own father being near seventy when Isaac, an only child, was born, rather his brother than his cousin and rather his father than either, out of the old time, the old days. (*GDM*, 4)

As in *Absalom, Absalom!* an enormous amount of information is stuffed into these opening pages of the novel, including the key fact that Ike has repudiated his birthright. We are also reminded of the Doane's Mill flashback in *Light in August,* for here again a large number of years are summarized in a brief, but powerful swipe of the brush, in this case ranging back before Ike's birth and the seventy or more years of his lifetime. But this opening brings with it an almost perverse countercurrent; ostensibly providing us with an expository account of Ike McCaslin and his family relations, in fact the passage deliberately scrambles those relations into an indecipherable array. By the time we reach the final lines, we have been led through a maze of genealogical terms. Although "father to no one," Ike does, of necessity, have a father, but he is referred to here only in passing when McCaslin Edmonds is characterized as "grandson of Isaac's father's sister." The thrust of the passage is to substitute uncles for fathers. Just as Ike has become "Uncle Ike," his biological father is called Uncle Buck, a man who, as we will soon learn, is arduous in his efforts to remain single and not become a father. It is as if Ike's displacement from fatherhood to unclehood opens a maelstrom of almost inscrutable relations that we can't yet map. Having repressed the father, the passage goes in search of a surrogate father and finds one in Cass, who is, technically speaking, Ike's second cousin. What makes the passage so gnarled, then, is the rhetorical energy with which it displaces and tries to deny fatherhood. Ike comes to us as "uncle to half a county and father to no one," and thus is situated from the outset in resistance to the genealogy by which he is surrounded and will never actually escape. Meanwhile, the usual genealogical track from father to son has been diverted, leaving both positions empty.

The story to follow takes place before Ike's birth, and in a sense, explains it, since his parents, Buck McCaslin and

Sophonsiba Beauchamp are almost brought together by the events of the story. (An earlier version of this story was called "Almost," underscoring the narrow escape Buck makes here, and only temporarily, from Sophonsiba's hunt for a husband.) But more important, the story provides a keynote to the novel's primary concern with race. Indeed, it is hard to resist the suspicion that every time Cass says "It was a good race," there is a pun intended (*GDM*, 5). The comic scene of the dogs chasing the fox through the house is repeated at the story's end, underscoring the story's basic plot device—people hunting people as if they were animals. Most obviously, Uncle Buck must hunt down Tomey's Turl, apparently a semi-annual ritual initiated by Tomey's Turl whenever he can get away to see his loved one, Tennie, over at the Beauchamp place. But engaging in this race for his slave puts Uncle Buck in "bear country," as Hubert Beachamp phrases it (*GDM*, 21). His sister, Sophonsiba, wants to marry Uncle Buck, and so is on the hunt as well. When he stumbles into her bed, he is trapped, at least until Uncle Buddy comes and frees him in a card game. The various comic ironies of the story are focalized by Tomey's Turl's being all too present, and yet brilliantly elusive. He succeeds admirably in winning the day, taking Tennie home with him, thanks to being the dealer in the poker game on which his fate as well as Uncle Buck's depends. Playing a classic trickster, Tomy's Turl exploits the internecine plots and counterplots of the whites to achieve his own romantic goal, introducing us to the black family whose past and future are to become the major focal points of the novel's plot.

The story aligns the hunt theme with the issues raised by race and slavery. Uncle Buck and Uncle Buddy, in an apparent effort to disavow their father's role as slave owner, have moved the slaves out of the cabins and into the big house, while Buck and Buddy live in a small cabin they have built nearby. Every night Buck and Buddy send the slaves into the big house and lock the front door, leaving the back door open for them to roam the county, until, as we learn later in "The Bear," "there was in the land a sort of folk-tale: of the countryside all night long full of skulking McCaslin slaves dodging the moonlit roads and the Patrol-riders to visit other plantations" (*GDM*, 251). No doubt this nightly dispersal of McCaslin slaves had something to do with Tennie Beauchamp's falling in love with Tomy's Turl in the first place, but it also underscores the ritualistic nature of the games played by blacks and whites both, as part of the mutual performance of the races before as well as after emancipation. When Tomy's Turl begins running away from the McCaslin plantation, he initiates his own form of ritual, one that exploits the white men's addiction to the hunt, and finally succeeds in forcing the McCaslin brothers to "buy" Tennie, thanks to the poker game that Tomy's Turl manipulates in "Was," set in 1859. In each of the stories devoted to the black family, a ritual is disrupted or reconfigured, but "Was" is the only one in which a black man finally succeeds. In "Pantaloon in Black" and "Go Down, Moses," the black man dies. Here, although he succeeds in his quest, the black Tomy's Turl is nonetheless cast in the role of an animal to be hunted down, even though he is Buck and Buddy's half-brother. Although they are essentially comic figures (their real names are Theophilus and Amodeus), their story introduces us to the fundamental guilt that comes with being a McCaslin and a slave owner, the guilt from which Ike will try desperately to free himself.

Ike's own story is not taken up again until the fourth chapter of the novel, "The Old People." It is the story, again, of a boy becoming a man, but one that moves in the opposite direction from that of Thomas Sutpen. Born into a patriarchal dynasty, Ike repudiates it in the name of the hunter's life. (Imagine an only son of the Planter who turns the young Thomas Sutpen away deciding to go up to Appalachia and learn how to be a mountain man.) In "The Old People," "The Bear," and "Delta Autumn," Ike's story unfolds in repercussive versions, but basically moves from his initiation into the wilderness through his repudiation of his birthright to the chilling exposure of his final inability to shed his racist beliefs. Confronted with the fact that Roth Edmonds has conceived a child by one of the descendants of McCaslin slaves, Ike calls her a "nigger"(*GDM*, 344). When asked what he thought of Ike in later years, Faulkner replied, "Well, I think a man ought to do more than just repudiate" (*University,* 189). The heart of Ike's story, as of the novel, is "The Bear," to which we will turn shortly. But first, we need to bring into focus the opposing figure of Lucas Beauchamp.

Juxtaposed against Ike's story is that of the blacks, chiefly Lucas and Molly Beauchamp. "The Fire and the Hearth" tells us not only the story of Lucas but also of the Edmonds, the "distaff" side of the McCaslin family that has inherited the land Ike repudiated. Lucas has changed his name from that of his forebear, Lucius Quentus Carothers McCaslin, shortening Lucius to Lucas; like Faulkner he derives his central sense of identity and power from his paternal ancestor. If Ike has learned to be a man through the blood rituals of the hunt, Lucas has become a man due to the blood ties he maintains with the man who was, at once, though unbeknownst to him, his grandfather and his great-grandfather, as if a special concentration of paternal blood had been vouchsafed him. He proves his manhood by challenging Zack Edmonds to a potentially lethal fight after Molly has spent six months in Zack's house taking care of his motherless child. As a "man-made" McCaslin, Lucas confronts Zack across the very bed he suspects him of using with Molly and shoots the pistol. Because it misfires, no one is hurt, but Lucas has prevailed (*GDM*, 52). "*So I reckon I aint got old Carothers' blood for nothing, after all*," Lucas thinks. In the eyes of Roth Edmonds, Lucas becomes a transcendental figure of fatherhood: "*He's more like old Carothers than all the rest of us put together, including old Carothers*" (*GDM*, 114). In the eyes of his wife Molly, however, Lucas at the age of sixty-seven risks not only becoming a fool but also losing his soul. When he sets out to find the buried confederate gold that all southern children were taught to believe lay hidden somewhere, he risks everything in a willful quest for wealth, even though he already has more money than he will ever have time to spend. What saves him from his own folly is his wife Molly's threat to divorce him unless he turns over the divining machine he uses to search for the gold.

In direct contrast to Ike, who tries to free himself of the guilt attached to his patrimony by repudiating it, Lucas invokes that very patrimony as grounds for the superiority he both feels and enacts in his social dealings with the "distaff" Edmonds line. He never addresses Zack Edmonds as Mister, and when it comes to Zack's son, he "did not even bother to remember not to call him mister," but "called him Mr. Edmonds and Mister Carothers or Carothers or Roth or son or spoke to him in a group of younger negroes, lumping them all together as 'you boys' (*GDM*, 113). Lucas unfailingly asserts his authority as a man and father, and Faulkner goes to considerable rhetorical expense in according him mystical status as such; as Roth sees Lucas, "*He is both heir and prototype simultaneously of all the geography and climate and biology which sired old Carothers and all the rest of us and our kind, myriad, faceless, even nameless now except himself who fathered himself, intact and complete, contemptuous, as old Carothers must have been, of all blood black white yellow or red, including his own* (*GDM*, 114–115). Displacing fatherhood from the white to the black family, Faulkner apotheosizes the patriarchal ideal, using the discourse of blood itself here to reconstitute the father in terms that aim both to eliminate the need for women ("who fathered himself, intact and complete") and to exorcise racial difference altogether. The fantasy at work: maleness trumps race. In real life, however, Molly can trump Lucas. When Roth tries to persuade Lucas to give up on the gold, Lucas stands his ground. But when Molly refuses to withdraw her demand for a divorce, Lucas finally submits, and the court scene in which he appears to stop the divorce makes us keenly aware of the racist contempt of the white men who dominate his world, no matter how proud he may be.

It is also worth noting that Lucas has already been outwitted by his daughter Nat, who has basically extorted a wedding and a house from her father. As Tomey's Turl tells young Cass in "Was," "anytime you wants to git something done, from hoeing out a crop to getting married, just get the women folks to working at it. Then all you needs to do is set down and wait. You member that" (*GDM*, 13). As in "Was," there is a comic side to "The Fire and the Hearth." Lucas is as canny as his daughter at certain things, managing, for example, to rent the machine to the man selling it, and to resuscitate his moon-shining business beneath the noses of the sheriff and Edmonds both. And of course the story as a whole celebrates the essential values signaled by its title, the values of home as opposed to wealth. But lest the potential sentimentality of this theme linger, Faulkner immediately hurls "Pantaloon in Black" at us.

"Pantaloon in Black" is often identified as a story that doesn't quite fit into the scheme of the novel. Rider, the central charac-ter, is neither a McCaslin nor a Beauchamp, and his story seems discrete. However, Rider and his wife Mannie follow the exam-ple of Lucas and Molly, building "a fire on the hearth on their wedding night," and Mannie's death opens an abyss of grief in Rider that enables us to recognize the force of the kind of love that makes Lucas bound to Molly in the end (*GDM*, 134). Read as a counterpoint and sequel to "The Fire and the Hearth," "Pantaloon in Black" reiterates the theme of love in the stark mode of grief. In so doing, further, it provides the novel's most direct and powerful response to the question of love that Ike will pose in section four of "The Bear" when he finds that the patriarch, L.Q.C. McCaslin, having slept with his own black daughter, leaves a thousand-dollar legacy to her son, Tomey's Turl: *"So I reckon that was cheaper than saying My son to a nigger. . . . Even if My Son wasn't but just two words. But there must have been love (GDM, 258).* Like Quentin and Shreve as they become Henry and Bon, Ike is driven to find love some-where in the history he reads off the plantation ledgers, but he can only find grief, and when he finds it, he cannot really imagine it. Envisioning Eunice's suicide, "on that Christmas day six months before her daughter's and her lover's . . . child was born," Ike imagines her as "solitary, inflexible, griefless, ceremonial, in formal and succinct repudiation of grief and despair who had already had to repudiate belief and hope" (*GDM*, 259). "Pantaloon in Black" imagines that grief, and thus both locates and authenticates the love that it presupposes. Understood in these terms, the story works as a startlingly brilliant prism, reflecting what is at stake not only in Ike's failed quest, but in Faulkner's as well, for *Go Down Moses* itself exacts a quest to overcome racism that is doomed from the start. If we take some time to understand this story, then, it will help us to see the starkly tragic racial impasse at the novel's heart.

"Pantaloon" refers to a stock figure in the Commedia dell'Arte tradition, typically a pretentious buffoon who is always being duped. "Pantaloon in Black" recasts this figure in the context of the American blackface minstrel tradition, but with a deeply ironic twist. In minstrel and vaudeville tradition the pantaloon figure becomes the stereotypical "Kingfish," of Amos and Andy, an older black man whose self-importance is always undermined, making him the butt of the joke and simultaneously reaffirming the racist view that he is a fool. The deputy who tells his wife the story of Rider's capture and lynching in part two of the story shares this view, describing Rider's behavior as beastlike, so wild and inexplicable is it. But the deputy himself is reduced to a kind of vaudeville character in the process; certainly he is an object of ridicule in his wife's eyes. "Now you take this one today," he begins, but she cuts him off with the quick stage joke, "I wish you would" (*GDM*, 150). He perseveres, however, because he's got a tale to tell, a tall tale. It's about a man whose behavior is so outrageous that it can't be explained save by an appeal to the most fundamental racist stereotype, that of a beast, one amongst a "herd of wild buffaloes" (*GDM*, 150). The deputy is not interested in the story of the lynching itself; that is literally a foregone conclusion, since the omniscient narrator has reported it in the opening sentence of part two. He is interested in Rider's astonishing behavior, and he makes a good story out of it, no matter how dismissive his wife may be. In order to assess that story, however, we must situate it in relation to the quite different story told in part one.

Pitted against the deputy's story is the narrator's. In a sense, Faulkner is telling a tall tale as well, but one rooted in black folk legend rather than the minstrel tradition. At "over six feet" and "better than 200 pounds," Rider is a reincarnation of the legendary ex-slave John Henry, the "steel-driving man" who proved himself stronger than a steam drill but died as a result of the battle. Rider's final performance at the lumber mill consists in single-handedly lifting a huge log off the truck bed and heaving it "spinning, crashing and thundering down the incline" (*GDM*, 142). But if Rider has the lineaments of a legendary hero, he is nevertheless intensely human. This is after all no tall tale. Not even Henry James could have put us so intimately inside the consciousness of a character. From start to finish of part one, the world comes to us exclusively through Rider's experience of it as the scene of unbearable loss.

When he walks home after his wife's funeral, we are wrapped inside of him as he steps into the lane:

It was empty at this hour of Sunday evening...the pale, powder-light, powder-dry dust of August *from which* the long week's marks of hoof and wheel had been blotted by the strolling and unhurried Sunday shoes, *with somewhere beneath them,* vanished but not gone, fixed and held in the annealing dust, the narrow splay-toed prints of his wife's bare feet *where on Saturday afternoons* she would walk to the commissary to buy their next week's supplies *while* he took his bath; himself, his own prints, *setting* the period now as he strode on, *moving* almost as fast as a smaller man could have trotted, his body *breasting the air* her body had vacated, his eyes *touching the objects*—post and tree and field and house and hill—her eyes had lost. (*GDM*, 133; emphasis added)

This remarkable passage, I hope, may serve to illustrate how Faulkner creates and sustains an intimacy between the reader and Rider which compels us to imagine that we are sharing, as Faulkner so often liked to put it, the very air that he breathes. Though here the primary medium is dust. The first sentence, even when abbreviated, as here, seems long, but it is actually a miracle of economy once we appreciate the distance it covers.

Focusing on the dust-laden street, Faulkner peels back its layered surfaces. Beneath the shoeprints of the Sunday shoes lie the hoof and wheel tracks of the wagons and horses, and beneath these lie the "vanished but not gone" prints of Mannie's "splay-toed" feet, left as she walked over this road to the commissary every Saturday. By means of a series of subordinate clauses marked by "which, "with," where," and "while," the sentence takes us back into the time when Mannie was alive, not just a yesterday, but a habitual time punctuated by Saturday afternoons. The serial metaphor of prints, from wheel marks to shoes to bare feet, works to bring into palpable form the presence of what is palpably missing. For Rider, Mannie's bare feet have left marks that can't be seen, but nevertheless are "fixed and held in the annealing dust." A memory of six months of Saturday afternoons is conjured up out of the dust. Then, in the second sentence, we return to the present, by reference to Rider's own prints, the metaphor turned now to become a marker of pace and speed, as the sentence uses gerunds to mark his steady movement, "setting the period," "moving," "breasting the air." Finally Mannie is conjured up again, first through the image of the "air her body had vacated," and then through the objects she can no longer see. The entire description is focused by Mannie's absence, and yet makes her almost as alive for us as she once was for Rider.[8]

In every moment of the story as told by the omniscient narrator of part one, Rider's experience of grief is represented with the same sustained intensity of focus we see at work in this passage. A sense of doom has settled over the story well before Rider arrives at the dice game announcing "Ah'm snakebit and bound to die" (*GDM*, 147). Although we may be surprised that he has a razor, we are not surprised at what he does with it, given what we have witnessed him experience over the previous day and a half. Nor, I would argue, do we judge him for killing Birdsong, the white night-watchman with the crooked dice. It is not only a question of justice, but also of fate.

Given part one, then, the deputy's opening claim that "niggers" lack "the normal human feelings and sentiments of human beings," is particularly stupid (*GDM*, 150). It is also jarring. The shift from tragedy to farce is too extreme. In telling his story about Rider, the deputy does bring into view the whole social structure of lynching, enabling us to focus our outrage at his blindness on the white culture that demands and supports it. But there remains an asymmetry between the story of grief and the story of racist violence and stupidity. The one leaves us with an unassailable knowledge of Rider's humanity, the other with the display of an ironclad social faith in his bestiality. For example, when Rider "grabs holt of that steel-barred door and rips it out of the wall, bricks, hinges, and all," bedlam ensues. We know why Rider cannot bear to be locked up; his breathing and need for air are a leitmotif of part one. But here, he is seen by the deputy as an animal bayed. As Rider hurls members of the chain gang across the room, "every now and then a nigger would come flying out and go sailing through the air across the room, spraddled out like a flying squirrel and with his eyes sticking out like car headlights" (*GDM*, 154). We are reminded of the description in "Was" of the fox tearing around the house, as well as of Boon, sitting beneath a tree shooting at the squirrels, both scenes of wild animals entrapped and driven mad.

I am not suggesting that the two parts of the story don't fit together; it is after all Rider's story from start to finish, and his behavior remains consistent throughout. I am saying rather that in this case, Faulkner gives us all the knowledge required to understand the tragedy of Rider's life, and then juxtaposes that against all the knowledge required to see that he will never be recognized as human by the white men around him. And I am suggesting, further, that the novel as a whole is invested in almost a life-against-death struggle to overcome the contradiction posed by these two kinds of knowledge. At heart, what is needed, as so often in Faulkner's work, is recognition. Recall the young Sutpen at the planter's door, or the serial ordeal of Joe Christmas, or the plight of Lucas Beauchamp in the white man's courtroom: each is denied his claim to matter as a human being. When as a young husband Lucas challenges Zack Edmonds, he thinks "How to God . . . can a black man ask a white man to please not lay down with his black wife? And even if he could ask it, how to God can the white man promise he wont?"(*GDM*, 58). What Lucas fully understands is that despite the careful terms on which he is working out his status in relation to the white man's world, he will never be recognized for the man he knows himself to be.

The same quest is at work in the story of Ike McCaslin. Ike sets out to emulate Christ in somehow redeeming the world. By bringing the dynasty to a close, repudiating his heritage, Ike—named after Abraham's son Isaac, to whom God promised His covenant—undertakes to initiate, even if only as a symbol, a new world in which race will no longer divide man from man. But Ike fails, his moral relapse marked by a failure of recognition of another as human. As the woman of "Delta Autumn" whom he calls "nigger" says, "Old man, have you lived so long and forgotten so much that you don't remember anything you ever knew or felt or even heard about love?" (346).

While he pursues the stories of Ike and Lucas in a quest (which sometimes becomes hysterical, as in some parts of Chapter 4 of "The Bear") to overcome the irresolvable conflicts their stories pose, Faulkner broadens the canvas from culture to nature, from history to myth, as if searching for a ground for resolution untainted, so to speak, by the sins of man. It is the novel's constitutive irony that he finds that ground in the wilderness, where live not metaphorical beasts but real ones. The only story written fresh for this novel, "The Bear," forces the racial impasse that the novel is always confronting back to a place and time before the fall, and therefore the scene of a possible new beginning. Although it turns out to tell the story of an ending instead, "The Bear" is a masterpiece.

There are two ways to approach "The Bear." The first is to read sections one, two, three, and five as a potentially free-standing novella, focused on a young boy's growth into manhood as a hunter, and the memory of the "big woods" as they once were before man destroyed them. The second way to read the story is straight through, including section four, in which case it is linked directly to Ike's repudiation of his heritage and is central to the novel as a whole. Section four, the longest section in "The Bear," brings Ike directly into argument with his cousin Cass, and into contact with his grand-father's history of incest and miscegenation. He has, in effect, two conversations—one with Cass and one with the commissary ledgers in which the McCaslin history resides. At twenty-one, he argues that Sam Fathers has set him "free" so that he may step out of the family genealogy into an alternative one, one in which Sam has replaced Cass as his surrogate father. Readers have always been split in their responses to this section of the story, some finding it the most profound and critical part of the novel, others seeing it as strained and overwritten. In my view, its being strained does not preclude its being profound. Its rhetorical intensity only underscores how much is at stake for Faulkner in his effort to find a way beyond the racial impasse: how to recognize the blood ties between races with allegedly disparate "blood."

The hunt for "Old Ben" derives in part from southwestern legends and tall tales of great hunters like Davy Crockett and the protagonist of Thomas Bang Thorpe's story, "The Big Bear of Arkansas," one Jim Doggett. Published in 1854, Thorpe's story

is already lamenting the loss of the wilderness to the encroach-
ments of civilization, so when Faulkner takes up this theme in
"The Bear," he is in a sense renewing the recital, in its southwestern humor version, of America's oldest story—the loss of
innocence. Beyond these sources and resources, there looms, of
course Melville's *Moby-Dick*. Against such a backdrop, what is
marked about Faulkner's approach to the hunt story is that the
bear himself, and not the hunter, is the story's protagonist and
hero. Its major characters are described in the opening paragraph: "There was a man and a dog too this time. Two beasts,
counting old Ben, the bear, and two men, counting Boon
Hogganbeck, in whom some of the same blood ran which ran
in Sam Fathers, even though Boon's was a plebeian strain of it
and only Sam and Old Ben and the mongrel Lion were taintless
and incorruptible" (*GDM,* 183). The "two men" then are both
of mixed blood; Sam is a mixture of native American, black,
and white blood, and Boon is "white," but also part Chicasaw
(on his mother's side). Lion is a mongrel, but like Sam and Old
Ben, he is nevertheless "taintless and incorruptible." Faulkner
introduces the discourse of blood in order to eliminate and
transcend it. The tale is "of the men, not white nor black nor
red but men, hunters" (184). As with Lucas Beauchamp, whom
he had tried to apotheosize into a domain beyond racial
division, Faulkner here invokes the primitive blood rituals of
the hunt as dictating "ancient and immitigable rules" that
enforce a moral economy of masculine virtue operating beyond
and beneath those of either town or country, city or plantation
(*GDM,* 184). In this domain, it is the bear who has a name,
while men remain "myriad and nameless even to one another"
(*GDM,* 185). Maleness, once more, trumps race, and also

gender. The storytelling of the hunters takes place around a fire, but it needs no hearth. What matters is that "there was always a bottle present," and "only hunters," "not women, not boys and children" drank the "brown liquor" in it (*GDM*, 184).

Ike is initiated into this sacred realm of the hunt in a series of moments, each with its own resonant power. The hunt for Old Ben becomes itself legendary, as men from far and near gather each year to witness the annual attempt to beat him. But almost from the outset, there is a dread built into the story. We know that they will ultimately kill the bear, but we also know that once they do, the hunt is over, the wilderness is doomed; the potentialities of the rite of passage story are already embedded in a nostalgic regret. The story of Ike's apprenticeship to the "big woods" is irresistible, but part of what makes it so is that we know that it is doomed. That is, our identification with Ike's phantasmagorical journey to the heart of the mythic past, his ability to hail, as Sam does, the deer as "grandfather," is enabled by the realization already established before "The Bear" begins, that the pure and untainted hunt has long since been displaced and usurped by the impure and tainted hunt depicted in "Was." When in section five of "The Bear," Ike hails, not the Bear, but the snake as "Grandfather," the fall into a world of sin from which he has been fleeing, is all too clear (*GDM*, 314).

How, then, do we understand the relationship between the three hunting stories at the center of *Go Down, Moses,* which focus on Ike, and the three stories surrounding them, which center on the Beauchamps and other black members of the community, all of them introduced by "Was," a story that aligns itself with both Ike and Tomy's Turl's son, Lucas Beauchamp? One way of responding to this question is to focus on section four of "The Bear" as the axis of the novel, the moment when the crossing of blood lines is acknowledged as Ike reads the family history as recorded in the plantation ledger. This moment leads to Ike's decisive renunciation, and his ensuing quest to atone for his family's crimes against the black race. It also validates for him his earlier choice of Sam Fathers as a surrogate father with more weight than Cass. His argument with Cass in this chapter, then, dramatizes his renunciation of one surrogate father for another, his alignment with Sam's heritage as hunter over and against his patrimony as the sole white male heir to the McCaslin property.

Ike is in effect trying to substitute one genealogy for another, to install himself in a line that leads through Sam Fathers to some autochthonous and purely male mythical source of power that resides in the relationship to nature made possible by the hunt. But Sam's line is by no means pure, much less purely masculine. There is Ikkemotubbe, Sam's biological father, and there is the black slave to whom Ikkemotubbe assigns the role of father and husband before selling the couple along with their son Sam to L.Q.C. McCaslin. In thus substituting a black father for himself, Ikkemotubbe performs the same fateful act that L.Q.C. McCaslin will perform when he provides Eunice with a black slave husband after impregnating her with Tomasina. Sam is a model for Ike in the sense that he embodies all three "blood" lines—white, black, and Native American—but has transcended and effaced the black/white distinction in his lifelong devotion to the wilderness as site of the hunt, thereby aligning himself first and last with the pure paternal Indian chief. But even Sam is "betrayed," in what is perhaps the most tortured passage in the novel, "not . . . by the black blood and not willfully betrayed by his mother, but betrayed by her all the same, who had bequeathed him not only the blood of slaves but even a little of the very blood which had enslaved it" (*GDM*, 162). Sam may have "had two fathers," an inversion of Lucas who has two fathers in one, but Sam cannot become a father without passing on the "blood" of his black mother. Thus he is "himself his own battleground, the scene of his own vanquishment and the mausoleum of his defeat" (*GDM*, 162). Sam's life enacts a ritual embrace of the wilderness, and his death signals the disappearance of that wilderness, already announced in the final killing of the Bear. In trying to follow Sam's example, then, Ike only ends up revealing its limits as a strategy for facing the future. Ike sets out to emulate Sam's model with a devotion not unlike that with which Thomas Sutpen sets out to emulate the Planter in *Absalom, Absalom!* But here that devotion demands that he not only step out of, rather than replicate, the genealogy dictated by the white patriarchy, but also become an uncle and widower, rather than a father. In other words, Ike excludes himself not only from ownership of the land but from the responsibilities entailed by family membership. Although he succeeds in never becoming a father, he fails at escaping the sins of his fathers, as his moral collapse in "Delta Autumn" brutally reveals.

What other genealogies, then, arise as alternatives to the white patriarchal one that Ike tries so ardently and finally fails to disavow? There are two other lines, as we've seen. One is the "distaff" line descended from Ike's aunt, in a family named Edmonds, and finally represented by Roth Edmonds. The other is the Beauchamp line, descended from L.Q.C. McCaslin, but significantly enough, lacking the McCaslin name. Although

Lucas Beauchamp has struggled with great energy to make good on his McCaslin father's paternal force, it is his wife, Molly, not Lucas, who prevails. And it is the black female genealogy, finally, that prevails in the novel as a whole. This genealogy stretches back to Eunice, who commits suicide when she realizes that her daughter Tomasina has become pregnant by L.Q.C. McCaslin, Tomasina's own father. Tomasina herself dies in childbirth, leaving a son, to be called "Tomy's Turl"—a name that suggests the matrilineal line has overtaken the patrilineal. Further, when Tomy's Turl marries Tennie Beauchamp, it is his wife's name that the children take, that is, Beauchamp, not McCaslin. Although a Worsham, Molly Beauchamp carries forward the force of the same matrilineal genealogy, commanding the participation as well as the money of the white community to bury her grandson in *Go Down, Moses*. Most significant here is the unnamed woman in "Delta Autumn," whose son by Roth Edmonds rejoins the "distaff" with the Beauchamp line. The woman's namelessness, as well as that of her child, underscores the erasure of any paternal name. A descendant of the Beauchamps whose child once again crosses racial lines, the woman rejects Ike's racist response with a devastating indictment of his moral blindness. Time and again, from Eunice's tragic suicide to Molly's obstinate faith that the earth should not be violated for gold, to Nat's clever manipulations of her father, to the Delta Autumn woman's courage, it is the black female line that traces the line of fortitude. But the racial impasse itself remains in place. Faulkner dedicated the novel to Caroline Barr, the black woman who had raised him and his brothers. Both the novel and the dedication pay tribute to the enduring strength of black women, but neither can overcome the hard fact of racism that the novel tries so desperately to dissolve. Lucas Beauchamp's aspirations remain not only unfulfilled, but impossible, and Ike's guilt remains not only unatoned but compounded. Faulkner would try again to address the issue of race, both in *Intruder in the Dust* and in public statements during the civil rights movement, but he would never again portray the racial dilemma with the force and complexity he brought to bear in *Go Down, Moses*.

Four

SNOPES AND BEYOND:
THE HAMLET

The Comic Gambit

AFTER COMPLETING *THE WILD PALMS* BUT BEFORE BEGINNING
Go Down, Moses, Faulkner returned to material he had been
developing from the outset of his career as a novelist—the tales
of Snopeses. Headed by Flem, a sinister and sociopathic entrepreneur who rises from dirt farmer to bank president in the
course of the three novels devoted to the family, the Snopeses
are more a tribe than a family. They spread their prolific
offspring across the county steadily as Flem brings in one cousin
and then another to work at the enterprises he just as steadily
takes over, from the store, the schoolhouse, and the blacksmith
shop in Frenchman's Bend to the restaurant and finally the bank
in Jefferson. Faulkner had been telling Snopes stories for many
years, beginning apparently with Phil Stone, but continuing
whenever and wherever the spirit moved him. In New York
and elsewhere, Faulkner enjoyed spinning yarns about the

Snopeses, and he did so with such effectiveness that some of his listeners, unaware of the tall tale traditions of the old Southwest, believed the Snopeses were real people. The earliest instance we know of in which Faulkner wrote about the Snopeses is represented by the unfinished twenty-four-page manuscript "Father Abraham," composed sometime in 1926 or 1927, and published finally in 1983, thanks to the editorial work of James B. Meriwether.[1] "Father Abraham" introduces Flem at the peak of his success in Jefferson, but then quickly moves back to tell of one of his most famous adventures, the auctioning off to his neighbors of a band of wild horses from Texas. The story was later published as "Spotted Horses" (1931) and then still later incorporated into *The Hamlet* (1940). In the course of the 1930s, Faulkner tried fitfully to begin a novel he called "The Peasants," and published four additional Snopes stories: "Centaur in Brass" (1932), "Lizards in Jamshyd's Courtyard" (1932), "Mule in the Yard" (1935), and "Fool about a Horse" (1936). The Snopes clan was, in other words, much on his mind. It was also fully incorporated into his vision of Yoknapatawpha county even before he wrote *The Hamlet*. As James G. Watson has pointed out, the map Faulkner drew for the 1936 volume, *Absalom, Absalom!* includes "Varner's store, where Flem Snopes got his start" as well as other details indicating that Faulkner was well in charge of a story he had not yet developed into a novel.[2]

In retrospect, it is not surprising that it took Faulkner years to arrive at a point where he felt he could deal with the Snopes material. It was, for one thing, enormous in scope and potential, addressing the social and economic history of Yoknapatawpha from the 1880s through the 1950s in the end. It was also for him a contemporary history, getting under way during the 1890s, the decade in which he was born. When he returned to the Snopeses in the 1950s to write *The Town* (1957) and *The Mansion* (1959), he would bring the story up to the present time. *Snopes*, as the trilogy brought out after his death would be called, constituted a kind of ongoing chronicle of his place and time, and thus addressed events and observations always still to come. Most important, I think, the stories centered on the Snopeses trace a line of narrative that is fundamentally distinct from those pursued in Faulkner's earlier family-centered novels. With the Snopeses, he was following the rise, not the decline, of a family, and his vantage point was distinctly comic rather than tragic. Like his protagonist, V. K. Ratliff, Faulkner had been engaged in what he called Snopes watching all his life, and he had an overabundance of material. But only after the achievements of the 1930s did he feel sufficiently in control of his medium to do justice to his observations. *The Hamlet* looks back on many of the tragic conflicts of the novels from *The Sound and the Fury* through *Absalom, Absalom!* but with a keenly sardonic eye for the funny, the grotesque, and even the human. It is as if this deep vein of humor had been running under the surface all the while but was only now available for mining. *The Hamlet* is among Faulkner's finest novels, a point that sometimes gets lost when it is addressed as one of the three novels making up the Snopes trilogy. The other two novels, written over fifteen years later, cannot compare with their predecessor, written at the peak of Faulkner's powers as a writer.

Critics in recent years have disputed whether Faulkner's later work represents as serious a decline as has been commonly thought.[3] I am in sympathy with this view, but only up to a certain point. My own reading of the later novels, beginning with *Intruder in the Dust* (1948), leads me to see them as by and large less impressive than those published between 1929 and 1942. I would argue that although he kept working at formal innovation, Faulkner did not again achieve the kind of sustained brilliance represented by the works of his major phase. Indeed, I think he himself was continually disappointed by his work in his later years. Among the most moving statements of this disappointment is Faulkner's remark to a visitor who found him in his study one day in May of 1950: "You know," Faulkner said, "there were a lot of days when I sat and looked out this window and knew I was workin'. Now I sit and look out this window and know I ain't workin'" (Blotner, 518).

Yet Faulkner never stopped writing, and in every novel he produced until the end of his life, one can find long and recurrent stretches of brilliant prose. (I am reminded of a comment that the cultural critic Greil Marcus once made in conversation about the later RCA recordings of Elvis Presley, noting that even on the least distinguished album, there was always at least one cut that showed Elvis's enormous talent coming through once more. I realize the comparison seems strangely incommensurate, but take heart from the fact that Elvis Presley was, like Faulkner, from Mississippi.) The novels do not always hang together structurally, and they can become rhetorically repetitive, but even in the most ambitious, and thus the most disappointing of them, *A Fable* (1954), one can start reading at random anywhere in the book and find a rhythm and resonance to admire and enjoy. Writing *A Fable* absorbed much of Faulkner's working energies during these years, which is one reason why it took him so long to get back to finishing Snopes.

A Fable is a broad allegorical reworking of Christ's passion as replayed in the World War I story of the unknown soldier. A wonder of abstraction, apparently the novel proved at least as difficult to write as it later proved to read; Faulkner spent over ten years on it. Keeping track of this elaborate story was so difficult that he made a kind of story board on his study wall, with the days of the week as headings. (The story goes that he had to reconstruct this chart when his wife inadvertently had it painted over one day.) Although *A Fable* has its defenders, it has never attracted either the readership or the critical acclaim of his earlier fiction. As David Minter has shown, Faulkner was in part moved to write this long-winded allegory by his deep concern over World War II, which he saw coming, tried to fight in, and followed closely, as his stepson and his nephew were on the battlefront. The war seems to have disinterred his oldest, and youngest, fears and anxieties, generating a remarkable, and in some ways heroic, effort to write the ultimate pacifist novel. The explosion of the atom bomb, which he focused intensively on in his 1950 Nobel Prize speech, only furthered and deepened Faulkner's sense of despair at what human beings could, had, and might, do to each other. In that speech, he urged mankind to aspire to victory over his own basest instincts. As always bedfuddling his critics, Faulkner seemed to speak out as a humanist while writing as a misanthrope.

The Hamlet, however, helps us to appreciate that Faulkner was capable of both humanist hope and skeptical despair; the comic mode of the novel enabled him to exercise both perspectives at once. The result is a kind of *tour de force*. Faulkner liked to describe *As I Lay Dying* as a *tour de force,* a term which, for him I think, meant a demonstration of ultimate talent with no visible effort exposed (*University*, 87). And *As I Lay Dying* certainly proved to be one. But *The Hamlet* is yet another version of the same triumph, this time perpetrated with an abandon and gusto not hitherto seen on this scale in any of his work. With *As I Lay Dying*, Faulkner in effect said, "You want a perfect modernist novel? Here it is." With *The Hamlet*, he said, "You want an American Balzac? Here I am." "The Peasants," Faulkner's working title for the novel for many years, came directly from Balzac, as did Faulkner's inspiration for turning the excesses of his prose and his imagination to rich social and comic purpose.

The Hamlet is a far more deliberately composed novel than *Go Down, Moses,* driven as the latter is by questions without answers, dilemmas without resolutions. Although both are made up of earlier stories, *The Hamlet* falls into coherent, if not immediately obvious, shape, whereas *Go Down, Moses* records a mounting and irresolvable ethical struggle. In *The Hamlet,* the outcome is clear from the beginning. You know that your side is likely to lose, but in the meantime, you can sit back and enjoy the game. Despite its many moments of horror and sadness, the novel is Rabelaisian in both spirit and scope.

The Hamlet unfolds in four "books," each forming a cohesive narrative unit of its own. "Book One: Flem" introduces us to Frenchman's Bend, "a section of rich river-bottom country lying twenty miles southeast of Jefferson" named after the supposedly French plantation owner who built and once lived in the now rotted house called "the Old Frenchman place."[4] Unlike Sutpen, who "abrupt[s]" upon the scene in Jefferson, Flem Snopes quietly insinuates himself into the region's central economic and political organization, at the outset owned and operated by Will Varner. "Chief man of the country," Will Varner is "a farmer, a usurer, a veterinarian," but he is primarily the owner of every enterprise in the village from the store to the cotton-gin" (*H,* 6). "Flem" as a book relates the story of how Flem Snopes gradually and relentlessly works his way into power as Will Varner's employee, then partner, predictably displacing Varner's son Jody, a process that fascinates the villagers through whose commentary we follow Flem's sinister rise. Central to this storytelling process is V. K. Ratliff, a sewing machine salesman who passes through town periodically, each time learning more of, but also relaying tales about, the Snopeses. It is Ratliff who fills in the background in Book One by telling two stories about Flem's father Ab Snopes, whom Ratliff knew as a boy. The first concerns Ab's alleged barn burning, and the second moves further into the past, explaining how Ab became "soured" in the course of losing a horse trade with the outlander from Texas, Pat Stamper (*H,* 31). By the end of Book One, an entire world is in place, Flem's upward mobility is in view, and the ground has been prepared for a potentially endless outpouring of stories. Although Flem's rise constitutes the central action tying this to the next three "books" making up the novel, the stories themselves range well beyond Flem, in part because he brings so many other Snopeses to town, but in part because the world that has been established is so rich that it can sustain a theoretically endless process of storytelling. Most of the stories to come concern money or sex or both.

In "Book Two: Eula," it is sex that predominates, thanks to the figure of Eula, Will Varner's daughter. "Not yet thirteen years old," Eula's "entire appearance suggested some symbology out of the old Dionysic times—honey in sunlight and bursting grapes, the writhen bleeding of the crushed fecundated vine beneath the hard rapacious trampling goat-hoof " (*H,* 105). As such a passage suggests, Eula affords Faulkner ample opportunity for rhetorical enthusiasm; he makes of her a kind of immortal but still fleshed sex goddess, one whose comic dimension emerges as a result of the fact that "she did nothing" (*H,*107). We might describe Eula as a Lena Grove who doesn't walk, who indeed lacks any apparent drive, even for sex. She sits, whether in chairs or in back of her brother Jody on his horse or on the seat of the family surry, "emanating that outrageous quality of being, existing, actually on the outside of the garments she wore and not only being unable to help it but not even caring" (*H,* 113). The more inflated Faulkner's descriptions, the more plausible they become in light of the hysterical behavior of the two men obsessed with Eula: her brother, and the schoolteacher, Labove. Jody, acutely aware of and anxious over his sister's erotic irresistibility, insists that she attend school in the vain hope that education will alter her behavior, but he must get her there and back every day, since she refuses to walk. He hates the ride because Eula can't help "emanating" wherever she is, and he knows always that her enticing thigh hangs forth as she rides. Labove, a young man with a large future ahead of him, is waylaid by falling hopelessly in love with Eula. Although he has worked as a schoolteacher and played football to earn his tuition through college, he cannot make himself leave Frenchman's Bend even when he has his law degree, so infatuated is he with Eula. He doesn't want to marry her; he just wants "her one time as a man with a gangrened hand or foot thirsts after the axe-stroke which will leave him comparatively whole again" (*H,* 131). When he makes his move, finally, she literally knocks him down, an encounter from which she emerges "not even disheveled" (*H*, 135). Labove's ultimate shame, however, only comes when he discovers that his sexual advance has not meant enough to her for her to tell her brother about it. Like Sutpen when he realizes that his father doesn't care whether he delivered the message or not, Labove is crushed with humiliation when he goes to confront Jody and finds that he is unaware of the incident. Labove leaves town instantly and forever.

When Eula does finally lose her virginity, four different young men leave for Texas. Only one of them is responsible for her pregnancy, but all want to leave the impression that he was the one she chose. The situation that is centrally traumatic in *The Sound and the Fury*—Caddy Compson's illicit sex and pregnancy—is here treated in ribald fashion. Will Varner refuses to be alarmed at his daughter's circumstances. She is, after all, his sixteenth child, and furthermore, he is not surprised. "What did you expect—that she would spend the rest of her life just running water through it?" (*H*, 160). He promptly and efficiently provides her with Flem Snopes as a husband, a bargain from which Flem emerges not only with a wife but with ownership of the Old Frenchman's Place as well. Thus by the end of Book Two, Flem has displaced Jody not only in business but in the family as well. Son-in-law to Will Varner, he takes Eula off to Texas so she can discreetly have the child which is not his. But he will return.

"Book Three: The Long Summer" weaves together stories of sex and money, both now displaced into new venues where violence erupts. The mentally disabled Ike H-Mope Snopes falls in love with a cow. It may or not be the cow that the widower, Jack Houston, has been feeding for the last year. This cow belongs, at least in theory, to Mink Snopes, he of the single eyebrow, who has let his yearling wander across the borders of his tenant farm to eat in Houston's pasture. When Mink tries to reclaim his cow, Houston refuses. Mink takes Houston to court, legally assisted by his proverb-quoting schoolteacher cousin I. O. Snopes; Mink loses, and is instructed that he must pay Houston three dollars pasturage before reclaiming his property. Mink instead kills Houston. Meanwhile, Ike Snopes has had a long and delicious lyric interlude with his love object, the cow. After he discovers that Lump Snopes is running a voyeur exhibition of Ike having sex with the cow, Ratliff puts a stop to the show, calling on Whitfield, the minister we know from *As I Lay Dying,* to advise a solution to bestiality. The cow is slaughtered, the meat fed to Ike in the belief that it will cure him of his bestial tendencies. Eck Snopes, the blacksmith, provides Ike with a toy cow to compensate. The end of Book Three finds Mink waiting in jail, hoping his cousin Flem will return from Texas and manipulate his liberation from a murder sentence. We know better.

A summary such as this one can only serve to set in relief the preposterously fertile imagination unleashed in this novel, and yet, even more preposterously, kept always under control. If we think back to Faulkner's first Yoknapatawpha novel, *Flags in the Dust,* the marked mastery displayed by contrast in *The Hamlet* is clear. As Ben Wasson complained, *Flags in the Dust* was at least "about six novels" and thus defied his editorial effort to refocus it as a single text (Blotner, 223). *The Hamlet* orchestrates a host of stories and characters into a thematically integrated suite. In part, what enables Faulkner to accomplish such formal coherence is the narrative spine provided by the rise of Flem Snopes, but what enables the novel's inventive scope is the genre of the tall tale. Each story outstrips the last in its stylistic as well as its thematic daring, in accord with the basic drive of the tall tale—to spin the story out as far as it will go and thereby to win the kind of competition in which Faulkner had indulged with Sherwood Anderson years earlier. Thus, for example, one might think the portrayal of Eula sets the limit for lush romantic prose, but then one comes to Ike's beloved cow, "the flowing immemorial female" whose movement Ike experiences as "the slow planting and the plopping suck of each deliberate cloven mud-spreading hoof, invisible still in the mist loud with its hymeneal choristers" (*H,* 183). Or again, one might think that the story about Ab Snopes's valiant but doomed horse-trading adventure defines an extreme; after all Ab ends up, after several swaps in each of which he loses ground, with a milk-separator but no cow to provide the milk. But the next time a Texas horse trader appears, the tale gets even taller. In the "Spotted Horses" episode in "Book Four: The Peasants," virtually the entire male population of French-man's Bend gives into the irresistible appeal of buying horses so wild they cannot be caught. The novel propels itself forward, in other words, not only by tracking Flem, but more importantly by indulging ever more aggressively in what Mark Twain liked to call telling "stretchers." Indeed, Flem's mysterious doings fuel the tale-telling process. To keep up with Flem Snopes, in other words, one must stretch the imagination to hitherto unexpected heights.

It is thus appropriate that Ratliff, the storyteller par excellence, pits himself in a competition with Flem Snopes, a man who rarely speaks but whose acts have increasingly serious consequences. Flem's conversational style is marked by brief, cryptic statements punctuated by choicely focused spits. He chews tobacco constantly but says almost nothing. As one of the townspeople puts it, "Flem Snopes don't even tell himself what he is up to. Not if he was laying in bed with himself in a empty house in the dark of the moon" (*H*, 309). Ratliff, by contrast, finds it difficult to stop talking, especially at those moments when he has just learned about the latest Snopes activity. But like Addie Bundren, Ratliff knows how words go straight up in the air while doing goes terribly along the earth. He tries to take action, first attempting to beat Flem in a complicated trade involving goats, then, more effectively, stopping the display of Ike's sexual performances with his cow. But in the end, of course, Flem gets the better of him.

Among the finest stories in the novel is the spotted horses story that begins "Book Four: The Peasants." Although the story marks the return of Flem from Texas, he vanishes from sight almost as soon as he appears, playing his usual role as a behind-the-scenes manipulator whose business no one knows. In this instance, Flem has arrived with a herd of wild horses to auction off, but it is not Flem, but Buck Hipps, a Texas horse trader, who does the auctioning. Flem thereby maintains his distance and can later disclaim any ownership of the horses, although it is clear from the outset that he will profit from the sale. The story, whose first telling goes back as we have seen to the start of Faulkner's career as a novelist, provides a kind of capstone and summary version of the tall tales preceding it in *The Hamlet*. It both tops them and stretches itself out to the maximum degree of nerve and time, revisiting and incorporating many of the novel's themes. More concerned with money than with sex, the spotted horses story nevertheless encapsulates both the resistance and the capitulation of women in the culture of Frenchman's Bend. More fundamentally, it illustrates the logical conclusion to which the novel's economic story leads: desire can be stimulated for commodities in virtually exact proportion to their uselessness, indeed even to their danger.

The men who are sucked into buying these wild horses (one of which we have already seen in action as Jewel's horse in *As I Lay Dying*), are poor. Most of them are tenant farmers working Will Varner's, or increasingly, Flem Snopes's land. But among them is Eck Snopes, Flem's cousin and now the local blacksmith, adumbrating the locally outrageous fact that Flem is willing to betray his own blood in the pursuit of money. In part the story's remarkable power comes from the sense of sheer inevitability that it instills early and often; these men are doomed. But it is the wives who pay, and whose children's interests and livelihood are put at risk and lost in the men's rabid bargaining. Flem's rapaciousness is nowhere else in the novel so vividly represented as here, where he is largely absent from the scene. Even his accomplice, the Texan Buck Hipps, proves unable to live up to Flem's standards of greed and inhumanity. But what makes the story live is not its moral; it is those horses.

Introduced as "a considerable string of obviously alive objects which in the levelling sun resembled vari-sized and -colored tatters torn at random from large bill boards—circus posters, say—attached to the rear of the wagon and inherent with its own separate and collective motion, like the tail of a kite," the herd of horses becomes, at least for a while, the central player in the story (*H*, 299). Bound together by barbed-wire, they first move as one: "calico-coated, small-bodied, with delicate legs and pink faces in which their mismatched eyes rolled wild and subdued, they huddled, gaudy motionless and alert, wild as deer, deadly as rattlesnakes, quiet as doves" (*H*, 300). Once detached from each other, the horses race back and forth within the fenced lot like the wild animals they indeed are, while Buck moves among them at great risk to life and limb, demonstrating that one might possibly survive owning one of them, but notably failing to demonstrate that one might actually catch one of them.

Ugly and misshapen (one of their heads resembles an "ironing board"), the horses embody the wild and untethered masculine power the poor farmers lack and seek (*H*, 302). The deadly but uncertain threat they pose to family is repeatedly enacted as Eck's son stands in their way, and yet miraculously survives each time. The graver dimension of this threat is realized in Henry Armstid's insistence on spending the five dollars his wife has saved on one of the horses. Mrs. Armstid has carefully stored up nickels and dimes, hoping to buy her children shoes for the winter. She has earned this money weaving saleable items, after dark, using thread given her by women in the town. Mrs. Armstid's frantic effort to recoup the five dollars her husband has so willfully spent catalyzes the entire novel's attention to the condition of poverty in which most of Frenchman Bend's citizens live.

The focus in *The Hamlet* on shoes, or rather their lack, as a signifier of class is remarkable, recalling the young Thomas Sutpen's fascination with the fact that the planter has shoes he doesn't even bother to wear. Labove, for example, comes to

Will Varner's attention as a possible schoolteacher largely because of the gym shoes Varner notices Labove's family wearing. Labove, trying to calculate the cash value of a football victory, decides that each victory adds up to one pair of shoes and therefore steals the pre-ordered football shoes from the football team's lockers and sends them, pair by pair each time his team wins, home to his family. Flem Snopes is characterized, among other regular features of his attire, by his soft-spoken tennis shoes. Hoake McCarron, the privileged class despoiler of Eula's virginity, wears "the first riding boots" anyone in Frenchman's Bend has ever seen (*H*, 151).

Set over and against the poor farmers is the exploitative economic development that Will Varner no less than Flem Snopes represents. The most fundamental class lines drawn in this novel are between Varner and Snopes, on the one hand, and the dirt farmers and common folk on the other. For many years, Faulkner was misunderstood as pitting the old Aristocratic South against the rednecks, but *The Hamlet* demonstrates clearly that his understanding of history was far more sophisticated than this view recognized.

For one thing, at the novel's outset Will Varner is already exercising the same credit mechanisms that Flem Snopes will perfect. Representing the generation that resumed planter control of the South after Reconstruction, Varner is well regarded as among the so-called Redeemers of the South. The only time Will Varner appears to get upset with Flem Snopes is when Snopes refuses to extend credit to his tenant farmers. Either Flem has not yet learned the benefits of the credit system, at this point, or more likely, he already aspires to compete with Will Varner as the county's chief lender. Either way, the system is in place when Flem appears to take it over. Ratliff can look back with nostalgia on the apparent innocence of the barter system that Ab Snopes played a part in twenty years earlier, but Ratliff is involved with, and finally outdone by, a system in which the miraculous flow of capital has little evident relationship to either labor or productivity. When Mrs. Armstid makes her plea to recoup her money, she says that she could identify each and every coin and bill she had saved. No doubt she could. But she finds herself in a world where money has become wholly abstract. That world may soon be dominated by Snopes, but Varner has long since helped establish it.

The final story in the novel, wherein Ratliff is outwitted by Snopes, has often caused worry among Faulknerians. How can Ratliff, the canny opponent of Snopes for the entire novel, be so simpleminded as to be taken in by the oldest scheme on the books? Flem buries coins on the Old Frenchman's Place, enticing Ratliff, along with the crazy Henry Armstid and the not so crazy Bookwright, to buy the property so as to dig up the confederate gold they believe they have discovered. Ratliff's fall is especially disturbing, since he has just proved himself apparently immune to Snopes by seeing through the spotted horses ruse from its very outset. The story may test our credulity as readers, but then one has to stop and ask, what story so far has not? And what else can bring an end to the potentially endless tale-telling? More seriously, Snopes's victory over Ratliff not only closes out the competition between them but signals the inevitable rise of the cash nexus as the central locus of power in the novel's world.

Indeed, we have not sufficiently addressed the distinctively dark side of this tale. While Ratliff rambles on, and we find ourselves serially amazed at the graphic depiction of both sex and violence, the tragic dimensions of the story signaled by Mrs. Armstid's plight remain to haunt us. Houston's tale is a signal instance. Racing in retreat from the "female principle" all his life, Houston finally succumbs to his love for Lucy, only to lose her as a result of his own stallion's attack. This is, of course, yet another tall tale, in the sense that a more aggresively Freudian story is hard to imagine. The "male principle" is enacted almost cinematically by Houston's deadly horse, not to mention his powerful hound. His own murder at the hands of Mink leaves him not merely dead but a decaying hump of meat, falling apart even as Mink tries to hide it by stuffing the corpse down the womb of a rotted tree trunk. Given the Freudian symbolism, it seems redundant that one of his arms has come off. Mink's own fear and terror achieve a kind of epic grandeur in the face of Houston's unwieldy corpse. Such a story reveals what all tall tales traditionally served both to acknowledge and repress—the material, physical, and horrific fact of physical terror, endured again and again in the face of insuperable doubt and threat. By stretching the truth, the old tale-tellers of the Southwest bucked themselves up and fought back their fears. The tall tale enabled Faulkner to push, and extend, the limits of his imagination, both in relation to terror and to hope. Ratliff may lose, in the end, but his cause remains articulate. Against the backdrop of Flem's ruthlessness, the Snopes family eventually comes into view as sympathetic. Eck Snopes and his son are already objects of affection for the reader of *The Hamlet*, and by the time of *The Mansion*, even Mink the murderer will command our respect as he returns from prison, to avenge Flem's denial of him.

It is noteworthy that Faulkner's full-scale comedy leaves the issue of race largely behind. Putting distance between himself and the central tragic subject of his work, he stabilizes the storyteller's role in V. K. Ratliff. Years earlier, he had found in the storyteller a figure of freedom from the restrictions of poetic form, and Ratliff affords him a kind of narrative leisure in which to play out that freedom. But Ratliff's downfall at the end reminds us that even the most intelligent observer and the most adept tale-teller can be a fool—if not about a horse, then about buried gold.

The Hamlet is among Faulkner's greatest literary achievements, and certainly his comic masterpiece. It is fair to say that no novel by Faulkner is wholly without moments of humor, but in *The Hamlet* he gave himself full comic license of an order nowhere else to be found in his work. Further, in returning to his earliest Snopes stories, Faulkner resecured his command over what he had now come to regard as his "own little postage stamp of native soil." The map of Yoknapatawpha County he drew up for *Absalom, Absalom!*, "William Faulkner, Sole Owner and Proprietor," he republished in a slightly revised form in *The Viking Portable Faulkner*, the volume that was to bring to a close the period of his neglect by both critics and the public.

The Public Years

What, then, do we make of Faulkner's life in its final quarter-century? With the publication of *The Portable Faulkner* in 1946, his fortunes began to turn. Thanks to a partly serendipitous, partly conspiratorial effort on the part of critics and publishers in the late forties, Faulkner was finally recognized for what he was, the United States' greatest twentieth-century novelist to date. As if to fill out the picture he and his new admirers had jointly constructed of him and his "postage stamp of native soil," Faulkner revisited Yoknapatawpha in *Intruder in the Dust* (1948) and *Requiem For a Nun* (1951), and also in collections of short stories such as *Knight's Gambit* (1949), *Collected Stories* (1950), and *Big Woods* (1955). He won the Nobel Prize in literature in 1950, and became a public figure, a role not always amenable to his temperament, not to mention his drinking habits. No longer dismissible as "Count No 'Count" to his neighbors, he soon drew their disdain on political grounds.

As the fifties proceeded, Faulkner became a U.S. State Department attaché, traveling abroad repeatedly to represent the virtues of democracy and the American way, meanwhile courting various ladies on the side. But the fifties also brought the civil rights movement, and Faulkner began to speak up. He made a series of public statements whose ambiguity has long been recognized. On the one hand, he firmly supported African Americans in their quest for social equality. On the other hand, out of his fear at what white racists were capable of, he advised blacks to "go slow, now." Accordingly, he managed to alienate both his hometown racists and the liberal establishment along with the leaders of the civil rights movement by insisting on civil rights for blacks even after announcing that he would, in the end, stand with Mississippi against the Union. (He later disavowed the last claim, made when he was drinking and apparently "channeling" Robert E. Lee.)[5] Although Faulkner was passionate about the moral and social imperative of integration, he was obviously still haunted by the same racial conflicts that had undermined populism and given rise to the Jim Crow South in the early twentieth century. His fictional treatment of blacks over the course of his career—and especially its growing sophistication from Dilsey to Lucas and Molly Beauchamp—provides a more reliable picture of his vexed concern with race and his deep struggle to come to terms with it than do his public statements in the fifties and early sixties.

As in his youth, Faulkner still found respite and relief in making up stories about himself. He liked to say he was just a farmer, provoking the famous David Levine caricature of Faulkner in overalls. Except for his encounters with students at the University of Virginia, where he was a writer in residence from 1957 to 1958, Faulkner usually found silence to be his best recourse in the face of his fame. At Virginia, although he occasionally got his own books confused, and often ducked innocent if daring questions from the students by talking on and on until he got around to a convenient moment for ellipsis, he nevertheless delivered intriguing and indispensable information about his view of his life and art. *Faulkner in the University* has thus become one of the richest resources available for Faulkner's readers. Faulkner's fondness for children carried over into his patience with students, for whom he clearly had more respect than he did for reporters. Since his one child, Jill, now lived in Charlottesville with her husband and sons, Faulkner and his wife Estelle spent much of their time here, and it was in Charlottesville that he wrote most of his last novel, *The Reivers* (1962). Although not in the same class as *The Hamlet, The Reivers* reprises Yoknapatawpha and its Snopeses, drawing in as well many other characters from his earlier fiction. A delight to read, *The Reivers* constitutes a nostaligic, comic coda to the many-volumned Yoknapatawpha saga. In a sense,

The Reivers is Faulkner's version of "The Tempest," a romance that refuses despair even as it reveals the grounds for it.

Faulkner was back in Oxford when he died on July 6, 1962. Although his death was technically due to a heart attack, his physical condition had been fragile for several years. In addition to the damage he had done by years of drinking, Faulkner had suffered several falls from horses over the years, leaving broken bones and other only partially healed internal injuries that caused him chronic pain. (He of course refused to quit riding horses.) During the final weeks of his life he refused medication for his pain, resorting to alcohol instead. But he was recovering from his drinking when he was taken to the hospital because of his pain. Asked if he wanted to go to the hospital, Faulkner replied, "I want to go home."

By the time of his "rescue" from oblivion by Malcolm Cowley and others in 1946, only *Sanctuary,* of all Faulkner's novels, remained in print. However one assesses the reasons for the dramatic rise in Faulkner's reputation after 1946, there can be no doubt about its thoroughgoing success. Irving Howe's *William Faulkner: A Critical Study* appeared in 1952, and by the mid-sixties, Cleanth Brooks, Olga Vickery, and Michael Millgate had each produced landmark critical treatments. In 1963, only a year after his death, *William Faulkner: Three Decades of Criticism* appeared, gathering most of the important early essays on Faulkner in order to meet the increasing demand among students reading him in both high school and college. Faulkner's canonization was secure by this time, but our understanding of his work had only begun. In the seventies, Faulkner criticism was immeasurably enriched by several new books.

Among them, surely the most important was Joseph Blotner's monumental *William Faulkner: A Biography*, published in 1974. Another landmark during this period was John T. Irwin's *Doubling and Incest, Repetition and Revenge: A Speculative Reading of Faulkner* (1975), a book that opened Faulkner's work not only to a psychoanalytic perspective but to other forms of "speculative reading," greatly enlarging the critical vocabulary of Faulkner criticism. Donald Kartiganer's *A Fragile Thread: The Meaning of Form in Faulkner's Novels* (1979) extended the reach of formal analysis that Conrad Aiken, most notably, had introduced in 1951. David L. Minter's biography, *William Faulkner: His Life and Work* (1980) continues to serve as the most acute and perceptive study of Faulkner's relationship to his work. In the years since, a host of first-rate critics have extended the range and depth of our understanding of Faulkner's work. Among the most important of these are Andre Bleikastan, Phil Weinstein, John T. Matthews, and Eric Sundquist, each of whom has provided new and regenerative grounds for studying Faulkner's work. In recent years, more attention has been paid to the deep issues of race in his work and, as mentioned before, to the "later" Faulkner, especially as his work relates to class. The impact of Hollywood on Faulkner, as well as what he learned from working there, has also become a fresh issue, as has his representation of and relationships with women, on which Deborah Clarke and Judith Sensibar have been particularly stimulating. Faulkner scholarship and criticism continue to flourish as new readers find new readings in what seems to *any* reader, at first blush, to be an inexhaustible text.

If new readers find themselves overwhelmed by Faulkner, they are in good company. And I don't necessarily mean that of critics. Consider Eudora Welty, Walker Percy, or any of the other southern writers who had to compete with his legacy in their efforts to represent the South: they too found themselves first daunted and then enthralled. Or Richard Baldwin, Ralph Ellison, and Toni Morrison, each of whom found both inspiration and challenge in Faulkner's work. Cormac McCarthy has, most recently in *No Country for Old Men* (2005), made of the American Southwest a social and cultural world of its own, in some ways more horrific than Faulkner's Yoknapatawpha County, but no less resonant in its Balzacian ambition to map a time and place whose history resonates well beyond the borders of Texas, Arizona, and New Mexico. Latin American writers of the "Boom" have made it clear how important to them was Faulkner's imaginary county, especially Gabriel Garcia Marquez, whose Nobel Prize speech is a direct response to Faulkner's. Why does Faulkner live on so powerfully, both in the works of his literary heirs and in the lives of readers today? After all, Oprah Winfrey declared "A Summer of Faulkner" in 2005, putting three of his most formidable novels on her Book Club list. As one commentator J. M. Tyree put it, "This announcement amounted to nothing less than a sneak attack on the whole idea of beach reading." He goes on to applaud Oprah's injection of "the perpetually relevant tonic of faith in ordinary people" into a cynical fiction market. The declining sales of fiction today confirms the self-justifying belief on the part of publishers that readers don't want serious fiction. Mass market publishers thus pander "to a dumber-than-thou audience they help perpetuate, while at the same time lording it over popular culture with snarky reviews."[6]

Tyree is onto something important in yoking together a "faith in ordinary people" and the capacity of those same people to meet the challenge of Faulkner's fiction. One is reminded of the longstanding question of how we are to understand, say, Darl's and Addie Bundren's fiercely sophisticated language in *As I Lay Dying*, given their humble station in life. By breaking the rules of verisimilitude, Faulkner is here forcing us to imagine some of the Bundrens, at least, as people with rich, if forlorn, imaginative lives. Perhaps one reason Faulkner's legacy is so profound is that his radical experiments in language were grounded in the radical faith that common people are capable of becoming common readers in Virginia Woolf's fulsome sense of that term. And even more radically, perhaps, he believed that those readers who think of themselves as socially superior by virtue of their privileged status can be compelled to realize their self-delusion.

Certainly, to read Faulkner with care is to learn how to see through social pretensions of every kind, particularly those that offer refuge from moral and imaginative honesty. Faulkner may have clung romantically to the "might have been" of his failed military career, but he also turned it to powerful use in constructing the searing figure of Percy Grimm, a young man who has never recovered from missing the war and thereby become a fascist. What Faulkner here demonstrates is also what his work provokes—a kind of moral intelligence that works tirelessly to suspect as fraudulent anything that makes "good believing" as it is called in *Light in August,* but also, and in the process, celebrates the redeeming uses to which the imagination can, and perhaps must, be put.

A FINAL NOTE TO NEW
READERS: BIBLIOGRAPHY

Those just beginning their reading of Faulkner have much pleasure in sight. Faulkner's own advice was to begin with *The Unvanquished*, a novel made up of short stories published in the mid-1930s and relatively easy of access. Which is not to say easy of understanding. Which is, further, to say that wherever you begin reading Faulkner, you must be willing to delay certain forms of gratification for a little while. As I tell my students always, and occasionally have to remind myself, get used to not knowing exactly what's going on. Understanding will come, but the pleasure of confusion comes first. The language itself should be your first seduction. Try, for experimental purposes at least, the opening pages of *Absalom, Absalom!* Imagine yourself in Quentin's place, trying to ignore Miss Coldfield's conversation, but falling back inevitably upon the vision of Sutpen, who "abrupts...upon a scene peaceful and decorous as a school prize water-color" (*AA*, 4). Try to place yourself in that (always imaginary) situation of childhood, watching "Cinderella" or "Peter Pan." Enchanted.

Once seduced, plot your course, but keep it flexible. Wherever you have started, start over. Begin with the *Collected Stories*. Read around. Don't be bound by the categories. Then take off. "That Evening Sun," for example, will lead you to *The Sound and the Fury,* and vice versa. Whatever you understand of this novel, leave it on hold. (You are never obliged to finish a Faulkner novel; you can always circle back to it.) Next try *As I Lay Dying.* The Bundrens will astound and amaze, not to mention horrify, you. But you should now stipulate, even if you're not convinced yet, that they are in fact human. From here, there are several options open. Since it is set roughly during the same historical period as *As I Lay Dying, The Hamlet* might be a logical next move. Or you can just proceed chronologically, through *Sanctuary, Light in August, Absalom, Absalom!* and *Go Down, Moses.* Another choice is to read at random. For not necessarily Yoknapatawpha stories, try *The Wild Palms, Pylon, Knight's Gambit*—a collection of stories having to do with detective work. Another is to select out the hunting stories: *Go Down, Moses,* or "The Bear," by itself (leaving out Section 4 for now), *Big Woods.* Another is to focus on short stories alone, beginning with "A Rose for Emily," "An Odor of Verbena," or "Barn Burning."

From time to time, you may wish for some guidance. Faulkner criticism is, alas, as apparently limitless as Faulkner's imagined world. A brief and painfully edited list of some of the many critical sources that you might find useful is provided below. If you want to read about any particular story or novel, or just learn more about Faulkner himself, the best place to start your search is "William Faulkner on the Web," where you will find a well organized set of references and explanatory devices, including a "hypertext" version of *The Sound and the Fury*. Should you become an addict, I highly recommend attending the annual Faulkner Conference at the University of Mississippi, located in Oxford, Mississippi, itself, normally held the last week in July every year. Although scholars attend and give talks, the conference is, true to Faulkner's vision, a favorite of his common readers, both native and international.

Critical Bibliography

BIOGRAPHY

Blotner, Joseph. *Faulkner: A Biography*. 2 vols. New York: Random House, 1974.

——. *Faulkner: A Biography*. 1 vol. ed. New York: Random House, 1984.

Minter, David. *William Faulkner: His Life and Work*. Baltimore: Johns Hopkins University Press, 1980, 1997.

Williamson, Joel. *William Faulkner and Southern History*. New York: Oxford University Press, 1993.

FAULKNER WRITINGS AND DOCUMENTS

Essays, Speeches, and Public Letters. Edited by James B. Meriwether. New York: Random House, 1966.

"Father Abraham." Edited by James B. Meriwether. New York: Random House, 1983.

Faulkner in the University: Class Conferences at the University of Virginia, 1957-58. Edited by Frederick L. Gywnn and Joseph Blotner. Charlottesville: University Press of Virginia, 1978.

Lion in the Garden: Interviews with William Faulkner, 1926-1962. Edited by James B. Meriwether and Michael Millgate. Lincoln: University of Nebraska Press, 1980.

Selected Letters of William Faulkner. Edited by Joseph Blotner. New York: Random House, 1977.

Thinking of Home: William Faulkner's Letters to his Mother and Father, 1918-1925. Edited by James G. Watson. New York: Norton, 2000.

William Faulkner: Early Prose and Poetry. Edited by Carvel Collins. Boston: Little, Brown, 1962.

William Faulkner: New Orleans Sketches. Edited by Carvel Collins. New Brunswick: Rutgers University Press, 1958.

FAULKNER'S NOVELS (IN ORDER OF COMPOSITION)

Soldier's Pay, 1926

Mosquitoes, 1927

Flags in the Dust (edited by Douglas Day, New York: Random House, 1973; originally published in abridged version, *Sartoris,* 1929.)

The Sound and the Fury, 1929

Sanctuary, 1931

As I Lay Dying, 1930

Light in August, 1932

Pylon, 1935

Absalom, Absalom!, 1936

The Unvanquished, 1938

The Wild Palms (1939; original title restored, *If I Forget Thee, Jerusalem,* ed. Noel Polk, New York: Vintage, 1995)

The Hamlet, 1940

Go Down, Moses, 1942

Intruder in the Dust, 1948

Requiem for a Nun, 1951

A Fable, 1954

The Town, 1957

The Mansion, 1959

The Reivers, 1962

SELECTED CRITICISM

Bleikastan, Andre. *The Ink of Melancholy: Faulkner's Novels from* The Sound and the Fury *to* Light in August. Bloomington: Indiana University Press, 1990.

Brooks, Cleanth. *William Faulkner: The Yoknapatawpha Country.* Baton Rouge: Louisiana State University Press, 1963.

Clarke, Deborah. *Robbing the Mother: Women in Faulkner.* Jackson, University Press of Mississippi, 2006.

Fowler, Doreen. *Faulkner: The Return of the Repressed.* Charlottesville: University Press of Virginia, 1997.

Godden, Richard. *Fictions of Labor: William Faulkner and the South's Long Revolution.* Cambridge Studies in American Literature and Culture. Cambridge: Cambridge University Press, 1997.

Hamblin, Robert W., and Charles A. Peek, eds. *A William Faulkner Encyclopedia*. Westport: Greenwood Press, 1999.

Hoffman, Frederick J., and Olga W. Vickery, eds. *William Faulkner: Three Decades of Criticism*. New York: Harcourt, Brace, 1963.

Howe, Irving. *William Faulkner: A Critical Study*. (1952.) 4th ed. Chicago: Ivan R. Dee, 1991.

Kartiganer, Donald M. *The Fragile Thread: The Meaning of Form in Faulkner's Novels*. Amherst: University of Massachusetts Press, 1979.

Irwin, John T. *Doubling and Incest, Repetition and Revenge: A Speculative Reading of Faulkner*. Baltimore: Johns Hopkins University Press, 1975.

King, Richard H. *A Southern Renaisssance: The Cultural Reawakening of the American South, 1930–1955*. New York: Oxford University Press, 1980.

Matthews, John T. *The Play of Faulkner's Language*. Ithaca, N.Y.: Cornell University Press, 1982.

Millgate, Michael. *The Achievement of William Faulkner*, 1966. Lincoln: University of Nebraska Press, 1978.

Mortimer, Gail L. *Faulkner's Rhetoric of Loss: A Study in Perception and Meaning*. Austin: University of Texas Press, 1983.

Polk, Noel, ed. *New Essays on* The Sound and the Fury. Cambridge: Cambridge University Press, 1993.

——. *Children of the Dark House: Text and Context in Faulkner*. Jackson: University Press of Mississippi, 1996.

Sundquist, Eric. *Faulkner: The House Divided*. Baltimore: Johns Hopkins University Press, 1983.

Vickery, Olga. *The Novels of William Faulkner: A Critical Interpretation*. Rev. ed. Baton Rouge: Louisiana State University Press, 1964.

Volpe, Edmond L. *A Reader's Guide to William Faulkner*. New York: Farrar, Straus & Giroux, 1964.

Warren, Robert Penn, ed. *Twentieth-Century Interpretations of Faulkner: A Collection of Critical Essays*. New York: Prentice-Hall, 1966.

Weinstein, Philip. *Faulkner's Subject: A Cosmos No One Owns*. Cambridge: Cambridge University Press, 1992.

Zender, Karl F. *The Crossing of the Ways: William Faulkner, the South, and the Modern World*. New Brunswick, N.J.: Rutgers University Press, 1989.

ABBREVIATIONS

AA	William Faulkner, *Absalom, Absalom!* New York: Random House, 1986.
AILD	William Faulkner, *As I Lay Dying.* New York: Random House, 1985.
FCF	The Faulkner-Cowley File. Edited by Malcolm Cowley. New York: Viking, 1966.
GDM	William Faulkner, *Go Down, Moses.* New York: Random House, 1990.
H	William Faulkner, *The Hamlet.* New York: Random House, 1991.
LIA	William Faulkner, *Light in August.* New York: Random House, 1985.
S&F	William Faulkner, *The Sound and the Fury.* Edited by David L. Minter. New York: Norton Critical Edition, 1994.
Blotner	Joseph Blotner, *William Faulkner: His Life and Work.* 1 vol. ed. Jackson: University Press of Mississippi, 2005.
Blotner, I, II	Joseph Blotner, *William Faulkner: A Biography.* 2 vol. ed. New York: Random House, 1974.
EPP	*William Faulkner: Early Prose and Poetry.* Edited by Carvel Collins. Boston: Little, Brown, 1962.
University	*Faulkner in the University.* Edited by Frederick Gwynn and Joseph Blotner. New York: Random House, 1965.
Minter	David L. Minter, *William Faulkner: His Life and Work.* Baltimore: Johns Hopkins University Press, 1997.
NOS	*William Faulkner: New Orleans Sketches.* Edited by Carvel Collins. New Brunswick: Rutgers University Press, 1958.
SL	*The Selected Letters of William Faulkner.* Edited by Joseph Blotner. New York: Random House, 1977.
TOH	*Thinking of Home: William Faulkner's Letters to His Mother and Father, 1918–1925.* Edited by James G. Watson. New York: Norton, 2000.

Notes

CHAPTER ONE

1. *Selected Letters of William Faulkner*, ed. Joseph Blotner (New York: Random House, 1977), 47. All future citations are in the text as *SL*.

2. Minter, David L., *William Faulkner: His Life and Work* (Baltimore: Johns Hopkins University Press, 1997), 44; all future citations are in the text.

3. Blotner, Joseph, *William Faulkner: A Biography* (1-vol. ed.) (Jackson: University Press of Mississippi, 2005), 64; all future citations are in the text.

4. "Landing in Luck" was later published in Carvel Collins, ed., *William Faulkner: Early Prose and Poetry* (Boston: Little, Brown, 1962), 42–50. All future citations are in the text as *EPP*.

5. Robert Cantwell, "The Faulkners: Recollections of a Gifted Family," in Frederick J. Hoffman and Olga Vickery, eds., *William Faulkner: Three Decades of Criticism* (New York: Harcourt, Brace, 1963), 51–66.

6. Blotner, Joseph, *William Faulkner: A Biography* (2-vol. ed.) (New York: Random House, 1974), 2: 761–762; all future citations are in the text.

7. I wish to thank Louise Mozingo for pointing out the source of Maud Faulkner's wisdom, Margaretta Lovell for many crucial corrections, and the American Studies Group at Berkeley in general for their invaluable responses to my work.

8. William Faulkner, *Vision in Spring,* ed. Judith L. Sensibar (Austin: University of Texas Press, 1984), 25.

9. Quoted in Judith Sensibar, *The Origins of Faulkner's Art* (Austin: University of Texas Press, 1984), 13.

10. Cf. "The Hill" in *William Faulkner: Early Prose and Poetry* (Boston: Little, Brown, 1962), 90–92.

11. "William Faulkner: An Interview with Jean Stein," in *Three Decades of Criticism,* 68.

12. For "The Liar," see *William Faulkner: New Orleans Sketches,* ed. Carvel Collins (New Brunswick: Rutgers University Press, 1958), 169–184; all future citations are in the text as *NOS.*

13. William Faulkner, *Soldier's Pay* (New York: Liveright, 1996), 3.

14. Willliam Faulkner, *Mosquitoes* (New York: Liveright, 1997), 320.

15. *Thinking of Home: William Faulkner's Letters to His Mother and Father, 1918–1925,* ed. James G. Watson (New York: Norton, 2000), 203. All future citations are in the text as *TOH.*

16. *Uncollected Stories of William Faulkner,* ed. Joseph Blotner (New York: Random House, 1979), 641.

17. See Estella Schoenberg, *Old Tales and Talking* (Jackson: University Press of Mississippi, 1977).

18. Quoted by John T. Matthews, "The Discovery of Loss in 'The Sound and the Fury,' " *The Sound and the Fury,* ed. David L. Minter (New York: Norton Critical Edition, 1994), 370; all future citations are in the text as S&F.

19. *The Sense of an Ending* (New York: Oxford University Press, 2000).

20. See Malcolm Cowley, ed., *The Faulkner-Cowley File* (New York: Viking Press, 1966), 36; this is an especially useful collection of letters as it includes both sides of the correspondence between Faulkner and Cowley. All future citations are in the text as *FCF.*

21. Faulkner's full statement is worth putting on record here. "Beginning with *Sartoris* I discovered that my own little postage stamp of native soil was worth writing about and that I would never live long enough to exhaust it, and by sublimating the actual into apocryphal I would have complete liberty to use whatever talent I might have to its absolute top. It opened up a gold mine of other peoples, so I created a cosmos of my own. I can move these people around like God, not only in space but in time too." See "Interview with Jean Stein Vanden Heuvel," in James B. Meriwether and Michael Millgate, eds., *Lion in the Garden: Interviews with William Faulkner, 1926–1962* (Lincoln: University of Nebraska Press, 1980), 255.

CHAPTER TWO

1. Smith, "Three Southern Novels," in M. Thomas Inge, ed., *William Faulkner: The Contemporary Reviews* (Cambridge: Cambridge University Press, 1995), 33. Future citations in the text as Inge.

2. William Faulkner, *Sanctuary: The Original Text,* ed. Noel Polk (New York: Random House: 1981), 321.

3. William Faulkner, *Sanctuary: The Corrected Text* (New York: Vintage, 1985), 321, 324; all future citations are in the text as *Sanctuary.*

4. See Michael Millgate, *The Achievement of William Faulkner* (New York: Random House, 1965).

5. *Faulkner in the University*, ed. Frederick L. Gwynn and Joseph Blotner (New York: Vintage, 1965), 87; all citations are to this text as *University*.

6. William Faulkner, *As I Lay Dying* (New York: Vintage, 1985),43–44; all citations are to this text, marked *AILD*.

7. See Sundquist, *Faulkner: The House Divided* (Baltimore: Johns Hopkins University Press, 1983).

8. Cf. *The Anxiety of Influence: A Theory of Poetry* (New York: Oxford University Press, 1973).

9. William Faulkner, *Light in August* (New York: Vintage, 1985), 8; all citations are in the text as *LIA*.

10. Quoted in Sundquist, *Faulkner: The House Divided*, 93.

CHAPTER THREE

1. *Selected Letters of William Faulkner*, ed. Joseph Blotner (New York: Random House, 1977), 75; future citations in the text as *SL*.

2. William Faulkner, *Absalom, Absalom!* (New York: Vintage, 1986), 80. Future citations are in the text as *AA*.

3. Edmund Morgan, *American Slavery, American Freedom* (New York: Norton, 1975), 5.

4. William Faulkner, *Go Down, Moses* (New York: Vintage, 1990), 245; all future citations are in the text as GDM.

5. *Robbing the Mother: Women in Faulkner* (Jackson: University of Mississippi Press, 2006), 124.

6. William Faulkner, *Pylon* (New York: Vintage, 1987), 20.

7. William Faulkner, *If I Forget Thee, Jerusalem* (New York: Vintage, 1995), 287, 273.

8. I am indebted to my student, Mary Knighton, for first calling my attention to the richness of this passage.

CHAPTER FOUR

1. William Faulkner, *Father Abraham*, ed. James B. Meriwether (New York: Random House, 1983).

2. Watson, *William Faulkner: Self-Presentation and Performance* (Austin: University of Texas Press, 2000), 173.

3. On this issue, see especially Noel Polk, *Children of the Dark House: Text and Context in Faulkner* (Jackson: University Press of Mississippi, 1996), esp. 242–272.

NOTES TO PAGES 59–164   195

4. William Faulkner, *The Hamlet* (New York: Vintage, 1991), 3. All future citations are in the text as *H*.
5. For an adept account of this episode see J. M. Tyree, "As I Lay Reading," *The Nation* (August 1–2, 2005): 36–39.
6. Tyree, 39.

INDEX